THE LEGEND

OF

CONFUSE-US

Timeless Bathroom Wisdom
From the Ancient Scholar

LAURENCE GRANT

AR
PRESS

Paperback ISBN: 978-1-965092-72-9
Hardcover ISBN: 978-1-965092-73-6

1. Main category— Humor & Entertainment › Humor › Parodies
2. Other category— Humor & Entertainment › Humor › Puns & Wordplay
3. Other category—Humor & Entertainment › Humor › Cultural, Ethnic & Regional

Published by: AR PRESS

Roger L. Brooks, Publisher
roger@americanrealpublishing.com
americanrealpublishing.com

CONTENTS

To my wife Kim
my soulmate, lifemate
and main squeeze through eternity.

PREFACE

Like you, I care a lot about proper etiquette in both public and private bathrooms. Having an attractive, fully stocked, and sweet-smelling powder room is a source of great pride, while a bathroom that falls short in any one of these areas can be a source of great aggravation. But how do we maintain good bathroom etiquette so we and our guests will be delighted by the condition of these vital rooms?

Toward achieving that goal, a lot of the wisdom in this book derives from the teachings of a relatively obscure philosopher named Confuse-us. You might be asking, "Who was Confuse-us?" Let me answer this way: You have heard of *Confucius*, right?

The great Confucius, whose given name was Kong Qiu, lived in ancient China from 551 to 479 BC. Although he grew up poor in the province of Shandong, his rare intellect, great curiosity, and strong ethical values spread throughout China. Indeed, Confucius's teachings have shaped the moral principles of China for thousands of years. On the other side of the world, millions of Americans have been introduced to Confucius through courses in history and philosophy—to say nothing of cryptograms and fortune cookies. He was considered by many to be the wisest of the wise, and his teachings remain quite relevant to all of us today. Much of his wisdom was compiled by his disciples in a book of his sayings known in English as *The Analects*.

Just ten years after the birth of Confucius, one thousand miles to the west in the province of Sichuan, another philosopher was born. As scholars have never been able to ascertain this great man's real name, he has come to be known by his affectionate nickname, Confuse-us.

It is said that Confuse-us was the son of highly successful area rug merchants, and that he grew up in what would be considered an upper-middle-class home. Encouraged to apply himself academically, he achieved

1

unprecedented high scores in a discipline called Practical Philosophy and graduated at the top of his high school class at the tender age of fifteen. He excelled at playing two popular stringed instruments, the pipa and the guzheng, and was said to sing beautifully and even dance a little.

Confucius became aware of Confuse-us when the young prodigy was traveling with his family to his hometown of Qufu. After hearing Confuse-us sing an original poetic piece while playing the pipa, Confucius was filled with great admiration. He invited the young genius to live with him and his family, and some scholars have speculated that many of Confucius's greatest teachings were penned by his young protégé.

The two philosophers seemed to get along quite well for several years, although there were some signs of the rift that would come to define their relationship. While playing music together, Confucius was upset that Confuse-us would often improvise. In his diary, Confucius wrote (without naming Confuse-us):

> Student not play note as composer wrote
> He needs to follow, our time is short.

Confuse-us would later reflect on these less than harmonious jam sessions by writing:

> It is my honor to play with great master
> Yet some of these songs are plain disaster.

Undaunted, the two philosophers worked side by side for a few more years, and Confuse-us soon became second-in-command at Confucius's first school of moral philosophy. Things appeared to be going well between the two. The protégé got along well with Confucius's wife and two sons, and he even built a house next door to his great mentor.

One evening, after a lavish lamb dinner prepared lovingly by Confucius's wife, Confuse-us became upset at the condition of his host's bathroom. Papers were strewn all over the floor, and after a hearty dump, he was aghast that his idol did not provide enough toilet paper for him to wipe with, or any spray to freshen the room. Confuse-us, being a considerate guest, did not complain to his mentor, but years later scholars found this journal entry:

> My hero is greatest mind of the East
> But his bathroom not fit for man nor beast.

When Confucius was the guest at his student's house, he didn't like that Confuse-us had spent so much on bathroom supplies: plush towels in a variety of rich colors, loads of toilet tissues, boxes of facial tissues, several bottles of air freshener, and everything that could conceivably be needed for a relaxing bath. Confucius, apparently thinking that Confuse-us was spending his teacher's money and not his own, wrote:

> My student is showoff
> Spending hard-earned money on luxury items
> while millions of people are starving in China.

Meanwhile, Confuse-us could not believe that Confucius left his bathroom without even a courtesy flush. He would later reflect on his dismay and disillusionment, writing:

> Why man so great have such sloppy habit?
> He treat my bathroom like wild rabbit.

This time, scholars believe, Confuse-us confronted his teacher, and Confucius was quite unhappy about being accosted in this manner. He accused his student of being ungrateful, and therefore unworthy of teaching in his school. After Confuse-us left the school, Confucius went so far as to repudiate his student's bathroom teachings.

Shunned by the great Confucius and ignored by his peers, Confuse-us continued to churn out eloquent musings on the great bathroom-related issues of his day. A measure of his greatness is the relevance of his teachings to the issues of twenty-first century bathroom users. So while we still follow the much more renowned Confucius on other ethical matters, we must turn to his shunned contemporary, Confuse-us, for our questions on moral behavior in the bathroom.

Not too much is known about Confuse-us's personal life, but scholars have pieced together the following information:

- Confuse-us settled in Shanghai, where he married a beautiful professional Ping-Pong player. They raised two sons and a daughter.
- Confuse-us continued to philosophize about bathroom etiquette, and he left thousands of these teachings behind. These writings did not bring him much income, but his wife did well, and he gave private pipa lessons on the side.
- Confuse-us was a voracious reader, consuming everything from children's books to biographies to literature in multiple languages.
- As a musician, he continued to improvise, writing his own variations, including very creative, humorous lyrics.
- Until his dying day, he took great pride in having one of the most luxurious bathrooms in all of China.

Although by all indications Confuse-us was not one given to boastfulness, he was justifiably proud of the depth and scope of his teachings. During his final days, he was said to pen this short, eloquent saying:

> People who follow me are winners
> Those who ignore are bathroom sinners.

INTRODUCTION

This is not the first bathroom book ever written, and it may not even be the first one you've added to your library. Indeed, there are several books on the market designed to give bathroom users a few laughs, or a lot of obscure facts, while they are passing their time…and their gas. But there are very few books that speak about the bathroom itself, and there are even fewer, if any, that address bathroom etiquette in an enjoyable, yet instructive way. That is the goal of this book, as I attempt to follow in the footsteps of my inspiration, the wise philosopher Confuse-us.

Justification

Why am I the one to write such a book? Admittedly, I have never been mistaken for Miss Manners, or, for that matter, Mr. Manners. I'm just a regular guy who may be a little more attuned than the next guy or gal to the pleasures of a positive bathroom experience, and the perils of a disastrous one. And, I have had more than my share of both!

As an account executive in the nutrition field for more than eighteen years, I have been on the road more than Willie Nelson. With my long hours and extensive driving, I have drunk a lot of spring water and a ton of coffee, which of course have led to a lot of peeing and a ton of dumping. I have seen the best and the worst features of hundreds of bathrooms over the years, and these experiences have taught me much about the need for bathroom etiquette.

Mortification and Humiliation

Fear and shame are powerful motivators, and insightful teachers. We learn from our mistakes, and I have made some doozies. Let me recount just a few disastrous episodes that have taught me time and again about bathroom etiquette.

DISASTER #1: My (now ex-) wife and I were visiting her brother's in-laws for a weekend family get-together at their magnificent ocean-front estate on the coast of Maine. On the last day of our visit, we all sat down to enjoy Sunday brunch on their outside deck with its majestic ocean view. My wife was giving me the pep talk about being on my very best behavior. I didn't think that was necessary, but I promised to act my *Sunday best*.

After a sumptuous and very healthful buffet with lots of fruit and fiber, nature started to call, and I excused myself to use the facilities. And what fine facilities they were…the pedestal sink, the glorious paintings, the marble floor with a beautiful Oriental rug in the middle of it. I felt honored to take a dump there, and I had to drop a serious load—a major power-dump. I kept churning it out, taking in the ambience of this grand room and forgetting to courtesy flush along the way.

I finally wiped up and flushed, and then I watched in horror as the toilet proved unable to wash away my load. And then… Here came the high tide. The biggest log of them all, the flagship of the fleet, washed ashore right in the middle of the Oriental rug that I had just been admiring.

Does the word *mortified* begin to capture my emotions as I tried to tell my wife what disaster had just befallen us? Well, let me tell you— this was our first and last visit to this palatial estate, and I learned a very important lesson in bathroom etiquette that day: Always courtesy flush your load!

DISASTER #2: My date and I returned to her apartment after a very romantic dinner at an Italian restaurant. She was looking hot and we were both feeling good, but for that pesky gassy and bloated feeling that was starting to hit me. I was sure it would go away soon and that the worst that could happen would be that I'd puff out a little breeze that wouldn't be detected by her ears or her nostrils. It didn't work out that way…

As I went to make my move (on her, of course), that little puff of air turned into a veritable cannon blast! And I just couldn't come up with any way to cover it up…like skidding my shoe on the linoleum or opening the door to simulate a fart noise. I was dead in the water. My date recoiled, then shot me a look that I can still picture today. My profuse apologies didn't quite cut it (pun intended), and she told me she was "a little tired" and had to "get up early tomorrow." As you might guess, this was the last time I saw her—although I still see that look she shot me once in a while! It serves as a constant reminder that we are often presented with crucial lessons in bathroom etiquette, including: Always go to the bathroom when feeling gassy and bloated. And never break wind in any public situation. Especially on hot dates!

DISASTER #3: Arriving an hour early for my industry's annual convention, I helped my colleagues set up our company's exhibit and prepared to put on my best face for our customers, as well as for the powers-that-be within the company. Twenty minutes before the exhibition floor opened for business, our exhibit manager asked me if I could run to the other end of the convention center to get him an extension cord. Being the good soldier, I obliged him, not knowing what was in store for me on this very busy day.

When I returned with the extension cord, the exhibit manager informed me, somewhat apologetically, that it was the wrong one.

I dutifully agreed to sprint another mile or so in my business suit to bring the correct cord to him before the exhibit floor opened. Luckily, I returned to our exhibit booth just in time to hand out my company's promotional bags to the now-entering attendees. But by this time, all that running had produced prodigious perspiration. My hair was wet, my shirt was drenched, my armpits were soaked, and my butt was now incredibly sweaty and itchy—and there was no time to run to the men's room and freshen up. I had to tend to the public. But I also had other urgent business to tend to. What would you do? Here's what *I* did.

I carved out what I thought was an oasis of privacy adjacent to our exhibit booth, and I started to scratch away at my itch. It was a killer itch, and I began to probe my fingers as deep as I could to get some blessed relief! One knuckle deep, two knuckles, even three... My butt was starting to feel good again.

End of story? Not exactly. Unbeknownst to me at the time, one of my customers had come to our booth and was speaking with my boss's very proper wife, who innocently enough asked him if his sales rep was at the exhibit. Well, this joker, this wise guy who shall remain nameless but not forgotten, pointed at me and gleefully said, "Oh yeah, Larry's my rep. He's right over there scratching his ass." Fortunately, I didn't see her immediate reaction. But I died a thousand deaths when the story was related to me later by the customer and his wife, who had also witnessed my exploratory efforts. My humiliation was not in vain, though, as I learned another valuable lesson in bathroom etiquette: Never, ever scratch your butt in public, no matter how bad the itch is! In fact, when you want to put on your best face, never show your backside in a compromising position, as there's liable to be a wisenheimer with a snide remark to make your predicament even worse!

Identification

Learning from my mistakes, as well as those of others, has been important in preparing me to write this book and to identify many important issues of bathroom etiquette. One area that has provided me with lots of material is the lack of good signs in public restrooms. A particular incident comes to mind.

One afternoon, I was about to meet with the manager of a VIP account. I arrived with just a minute to spare before meeting time, and I needed to use the john. As I tore around the corner and was about to open the restroom door, I didn't notice a poorly placed sign, affixed with clear plastic tape, that read:

Do Not Enter—Please Use Other Restroom

How was I supposed to see that sign as I was rushing to the *Promised Land*? I didn't see it, and I remember my head literally snapping back as I attempted to undertake my mission. I could have sued for whiplash, though I didn't. But I did learn how important it is to give clear and legible instructions for the proper use—or non-use, as the case might be—of the restroom.

Verification

Ever since that meeting, it's been my habit to look for the best and worst restroom signs across my sales territory. I've taken photos of countless restroom signs. I've found humorous signs, instructive signs without humor, and many signs that were simply inadequate. I've also seen signs that were worded in such a mean-spirited way that they undoubtedly insulted and offended all restroom users with decent eyesight.

And then one day, when not even focused on my quest, I saw a stellar sign in a restroom that was clearly placed by someone who was tired of cleaning up after users with shameful marksmanship, yet had managed to retain her sense of humor about it all.

The sign read:

If you sprinkle when you tinkle,
Please be neat and wipe the seat.

This sign was poetic, instructive and humorous, and its message stayed with me. It also solidified my desire to create my own poetic jingles about all aspects of bathroom etiquette.

Education

Having learned, mostly the hard way, many essential lessons in bathroom etiquette, my objective was now to cover all important situations, mistakes, and remedies for the bathroom with poetic jingles. I wanted to address what really happens in bathrooms everywhere in a humorous yet effective way. It quickly became a labor of love, an obsession, and a kind of spiritual quest to help you, my brothers and sisters, learn from the mistakes I have made.

My goal is that my bathroom disasters will resonate with you. Perhaps you will be reminded of similar breaches of bathroom etiquette by yourself or others, and that those experiences will become your guide to learning and sharing proper bathroom etiquette moving forward.

I hope you will remember some of the jingles, song parodies, quotes, and ditties in this book, and that they will lead you to more fulfilling bathroom experiences in the future. I don't want you to lose your girlfriend or boyfriend because you cut the cheese at an inopportune time. I don't want you to jeopardize the sterling reputation that you have built in your profession, simply because you didn't take the time to scratch your itchy butt behind closed doors.

And if you, dear reader, are ever a guest in my home, you must always courtesy flush, so you will never float a submarine on my Oriental rug!

CHAPTER 1

CONFUSE-US RULES OF BATHROOM ETIQUETTE

Confucius was an ancient scholar whose code of ethical and moral behavior has guided billions of people over the years. Confuse-us, just ten years younger than Confucius, became his elder's protégé and friend until they stopped working together, breaking with one another over issues of bathroom conduct. It is important to note that the brilliant Confucius often neglected his own bathroom behavior. Nobody's perfect, and this was, regrettably, one of his few flaws.

The story of these Chinese philosophers is important for two reasons: 1) Breaches of bathroom etiquette can lead to the loss of friendships, the dissolution of work partnerships and even family feuds; and 2) We can continually learn from the younger of these scholars, who devoted the past twenty-five or so years of his life to bathroom etiquette.

Scholars believe Confuse-us maintained one of the finest private bathrooms in all of ancient China, and he was quite aware of his obligation to maintain it. He wrote:

> When my guests visit and unload their booty
> Giving them comfort is my solemn duty.

Still, it is remarkable that a man who lived in the fifth century BC was so attuned to so many bathroom concerns, including:

- being a great host
- being an ideal guest

- respecting one's elders
- men respecting women
- women respecting men
- important tips for maintaining good health and hygiene
- showing modesty at all times

Once I became aware of Confuse-us, my goal was to spread his wisdom and to use his example to expand upon it—which I hope will become evident in the chapters that follow. For now, please enjoy these serious yet humorous nuggets of bathroom etiquette wisdom from this great ancient scholar.

Confuse-us say...

> Confucius was great man, they say
> Indeed, had wisdom in his day
> But when not stocking enough bathroom spray
> I chastised him without delay.

Confuse-us say...

> When bathroom odor is very flagrant
> must spray air with something fragrant.

Confuse-us say...

> Even the lowest cad or wench
> not deserving to smell your stench.

Confuse-us say...

> Man needs to wear mask with no complaint
> when bathroom odor can peel the paint.

Confuse-us say...

> Man takes us down a rocky road
> when never flushing his nasty load.

Confuse-us say...

> After you wipe keep remnants unseen
> use moist towelettes to keep butthole most clean.

Confuse-us say...

> Bathroom not good place for meeting
> after flush and spray completing
> Find new room, for friendly greeting.

Confuse-us say...

> After from toilet disembark
> turn off light and make room dark.

Confuse-us say...

> Bathroom is business, not exhibition
> must follow old locked-door tradition.

Confuse-us say...

> Man who leaves seat up after use
> engages in subtle woman abuse.

Confuse-us say...

> Nothing makes man quite as mad
> as a woman flushing her private pad
> Throw in trashcan, all be glad.

Confuse-us say...

> Man not wipe seat of pee and poop
> must be banished from the group.

Confuse-us say…

> Host engage in great deceit
> when give guest broken toilet seat
> Fix it now, then room complete.

Confuse-us say…

> Problem I never understand
> Man do Number Two as planned
> and then not bother to wash his hand.

Confuse-us say…

> Who give you right to be so cunning?
> Jiggle handle if toilet still running.

Confuse-us say…

> Host not stocking spray and paper
> for guest to wipe and cleanse the vapor
> Make visit to home, a deal breaker.

Confuse-us say…

> When using bathroom, time well spent
> You not paying six-month rent
> Remember, there's waiting a lady or gent.

Confuse-us say…

> Host scrub and brush her floors and tiles
> bring to guests some happy smiles.

Confuse-us say...

> Don't piddle your pee without a care
> Always maintain dry underwear
> Stash extra TP, if only a square.

Confuse-us say...

> If man concerned with dripping pee
> stuff TP in drawers for dry dungaree.

Confuse-us say...

> When exercise heavy in summer sun
> man's case of swamp ass just begun.

Confuse-us say...

> When man drop deuce in public place
> man must get rid of every trace.

Confuse-us say...

> Man who wipes bottom with little care
> may leave dingleberries in derriere.

Confuse-us say...

> Man who farts while playing sports
> will leave brown skidmarks in his shorts.

Confuse-us say...

> When man wipe sloppily his rear
> man's rectal itch will be severe.

Confuse-us say...

When man fudge undies with streaks of brown
man must walk street with head bent down.

Confuse-us say...

Man who much too quickly wipes
leaves on underwear soiled stripes.

Confuse-us say...

Man must really scrub his fingers
if brownish smudge on hand still lingers.

Confuse-us say...

If man break wind in public place
his family will bear disgrace.

Confuse-us say...

The deadly fart that makes no noise
is one of some folks' greatest joys.

Confuse-us say...

When man shoots out some SBDs
man just might smear his BVDs.

Confuse-us say...

When husband puff gas without a warning
wife will have a smelly morning.

Confuse-us say...

> When man eat a lot of roughage
> man must control his deadly puffage.

Confuse-us say...

> Man who eat much fiber and fruit
> will produce one healthy poot.

Confuse-us say...

> When man eats a ton of tofu
> man soon needs to pinch a loaf-u.

Confuse-us say...

> When butt hair coarse like paper shredder
> man must wipe with thicker spreader.

Confuse-us say...

> Man who has a bloody stool
> must not pass gas in swimming pool.

Confuse-us say...

> When man wipe butt with extra care
> man feel happy everywhere

Confuse-us say...

> When man's butt has hemorrhoid
> man feel sad, and much annoyed.

Confuse-us say...

> The key to a good woman's heart
> is to suppress your stinky fart.

Confuse-us say...

> He who has bad bathroom runs
> need plenty of paper for his buns.

Confuse-us say...

> When man drop fudge like maniac
> man will strain man's cardiac
> When man slow dump his doody pack
> man will not suffer heart attack.

Confuse-us say...

> Man who will not flush his poop
> will find himself shunned by group.

Confuse-us say...

> Man who sits and craps a ton
> must flush and spray when he is done.

Confuse-us say...

> If man's turtle head begin to poke
> run to john, this is not joke.

Confuse-us say...

> When man needs to grow a tail
> man must run to bathroom without fail.

Confuse-us say...

When man eat power-lunch at noon
man's power-dump will follow soon.

Confuse-us say...

If man take crap and leave in rush
when man return, he'll cringe and blush.

Confuse-us say...

Woman who never flush her doot
will be held in ill repute.

Confuse-us say...

When woman leave room to powder nose
beware of bathroom stench she impose.

Confuse-us say...

Politicians who don't flush floaters
turn away potential voters.

Confuse-us say...

If man use public john at night
man must always turn off light
If man use public john by day
man must turn off light anyway.

Confuse-us say...

Host who keep bathroom dimly lit
have guest who is afraid to sit.

Confuse-us say...

> Young boy or girl should not take crap
> when sitting on an elder's lap.

Confuse-us say...

> When bathroom dryer leaves hands wet
> dry hands on shirt without regret.

Confuse-us say...

> Man must use napkin to turn doorknob
> to avoid fecal matter left by bathroom slob.

Confuse-us say...

> When man touch bathroom door with naked hand
> its lethal germs man won't withstand.

Confuse-us say...

> When man crumple paper towels
> and play bathroom basketball game
> man must rebound all misses
> or shoot paper with perfect aim.

Confuse-us say...

> Man must keep hopper in proper way
> raised toilet lid destroy Feng Shui.

Confuse-us say...

> Hosts who sit on toilet with open door
> will lose their guests forever more.

Confuse-us say...

Man who never returns seat to the throne
will find himself often sleeping alone.

Confuse-us say...

Man is only granted the right to cuss
when someone leaves poop on his porcelain bus.

Confuse-us say...

Those who suffer from constipation
have plenty of time for contemplation.

Confuse-us say...

Butt gravy after flatulation
makes for sticky situation.

Confuse-us say...

Good son's Number Two
leaves behind no residue.

Confuse-us say...

Man who never take clean bath
will find angry woman in his path.

Confuse-us say...

People who have sex on bathroom tiles
must leave quickly without big smiles.

Confuse-us say...

Man who makes love in the crapper
must dispose of condom wrapper.

Confuse-us say...

If man peek under bathroom stall
and see coworkers' slacks and shoes
man must not pay a business call
or coworkers' friendship man will lose.

Confuse-us say...

Man who swings on flying trapeze
will stumble and fall if he cuts the cheese.

Confuse-us say...

Man who army just recruit
may be shaking in his boot
if on his march, man need to doot.

Confuse-us say...

Man who in bathroom too long repose
thinks not of others and it shows.

Confuse-us say...

Man who bounce pee off urinal pad
will soon find clothing urine clad.

Confuse-us say...

Man is making huge mistake
if he eats the urinal cake.

Confuse-us say...

> If bum rush in and wants seat now
> kick that bum out, then drop trou.

Confuse-us remind...

> Leave no trace from your behind.

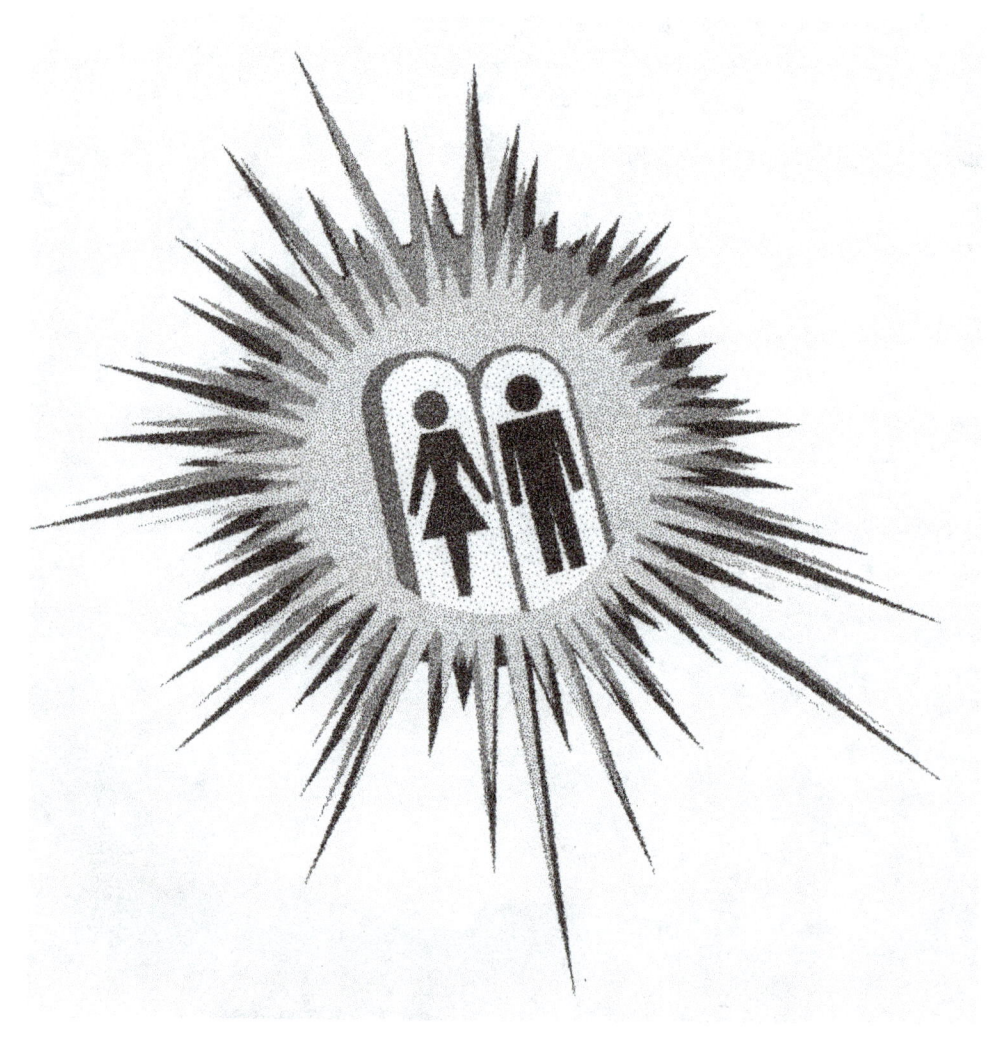

CHAPTER 2

THE COMMANDMENTS OF
BATHROOM ETIQUETTE

Guided by his mentor, Confucius, we are not sure if Confuse-us believed in a deity, but we have reason to believe that he was aware of the presence of the Ten Commandments, written centuries before his time. The commandments appear to have been an important influence on his moral teachings, which he applied to bathroom etiquette. Take it from the man himself:

> Man who ignore commandment laws
> May keep bathroom with many flaws
> Too dirty for even raccoons' paws.

He also penned this teaching, which is consistent with The Golden Rule.

> Do unto others as you'd want them to do
> Always flush away your poo.

Given his various teachings and journal notes, I am sure Confuse-us would approve of the use of commandments to illustrate the imperative of following good bathroom etiquette. Note that there are far more than ten commandments below, because how could we limit them? We should not. And we could not.

My hope is that these commandments will serve as your holy guidelines for proper bathroom behavior. Share these commandments with your family and friends. We certainly do not want to encourage any more bathroom etiquette sinners. Indeed, follow these commandments and thou shalt never be a sinner again. At least not in thy bathroom.

Thou shalt locketh thy door when doing thy duty
For thou shalt never exposeth thy booty.

Thou must cleaneth thy hands, please giveth some hope
Useth thy hot water and plenty of soap.

Thou shalt scrubbeth thy hands before singing my psalms
Washeth front and back both fingers and palms.

Thou must saveth some money
So turn off thy power
when leaving thy bathroom
no matter thy hour.

In foul bathroom odors, thou shalt not bask
So cover thy nostrils and mouth with a mask.

I giveth to thou, thy daily bread
So sprayeth thy room, and thine odors be dead.

Thou shalt stocketh supplies for all who may enter
Don't acteth a cheapskate, don't be so self-centered.

Thou shalt not leaveth a mess all over thy loo
Wipeth thy pee and each Number Two.

Repaireth thy toilet and fixeth thy sink
Leaveth plenty of spray so thy bathroom won't stink.

Thou shalt closeth thy lid before thou flush
Keepeth airborne particles off thy toothbrush.

Thy bathroom shalt not be thy congregation
No shaking, no hugging, no conversation.

Thou shalt useth towelettes for after thy wipeth
Thine ass will be happy, no reason to gripeth.

Thine underwear needeth to stay crisp and dry
Storeth extra toilet paper if only one ply.

Be careful of thy deuce thou droppeth
If causeth high tide, thou hast to moppeth.

Thou shalt not lifteth too heavy a mass
Or thy bottom shalt suffereth from swamp ass.

Thou shalt keepeth thy hands bacteria-free
Flusheth thy toilet with elbow or knee.

Thou shalt not breaketh wind without a care
or skidmarks will graceth thine underwear.

Thou shalt wipeth up fully, but do not stuff
or dingleberries will adorn thy duff.

Thou shalt wipeth well to best avoid
a bleeding case of hemorrhoids.

Thou shalt not scratcheth thy rectal itch
Wipeth again, and fixeth that glitch.

Thou shalt treateth thine undies with great compassion
fudging thine undies is not high fashion.

Thou shalt be subject to mine judgment
if thine undies show thine fudgement.

Thou shalt groweth thy tail with great care
or thou might staineth thine underwear.

If thou misses thy target with thy Number One
thy cleanup job has just begun.

Thou shalt be kind to thy fellow man
Sprayeth thy room after thou useth thy can.

After thou completeth thy dump
Thou shalt not leaveth a brownish lump.

When thy bowels start to inch
Thou shalt giveth thy loaf a pinch.

Thou shalt say, Excuse me, please
if thou, in public, cutteth thy cheese.

Thou shalt not farteth without a sound
or deadly gas will soon abound.

Thou shalt taketh thy time when dumping
or thy heart will struggle pumping
So crapping slowly still works best
Thou don't needeth cardiac arrest.

Thou shalt maketh thy poo
with consideration for others
who waiteth in queue.

Thou shalt not tie up thy stall with reading
while others' bowels may be bleeding.

Thou shalt sendeth thy stool out in thy mail
for thy doctor to check what's in thy tail.

Thou shalt keepeth thy bathroom nice and bright
Don't let thy guests crap without light.

Thou shalt shutteth thy light off after thy dumpeth
or thine electric bill will really jumpeth.

Thou shalt always wipeth clean thy bottom bare
Leaveth no smudge on thy rectal hair.

When thy rectal region loseth its friction
butt gravy shalt be thine affliction.

Thou shalt aim when thou pee, don't ever cheat
So men, don't even think of not lifting thy seat.

Thou shalt admire beautiful bathrooms
And thou shalt never covet
Pitch in and scrubbeth thy bathroom now
And guests will learn to love it.

Thou shalt not bareth thy private parts
Locketh thy door and showeth some smarts.

Thou shalt not leaveth thy bathroom looking squalid
Flusheth thy movements when they're solid.

Thou shalt remember to honor the next user of thy pot
Thou must flusheth and sprayeth
Little things mean a lot.

Thou shalt not write upon thy stall door
do not breaketh thy treaty
As God is closely watching
each sneaky writer of graffiti.

Honor thy mother and father
Make sure thou washeth thy hands
Follow thy Golden Rule they spoke
And protecteth thy fellow man.

Honor thy father and mother
and keepeth thy bathroom clean
Scour thy toilet daily
Make it the best they've ever seen.

Thou shalt not let thy water gusheth
Jiggle thy handle after thou flusheth.

Thou shalt not let thy toilet runneth
So jiggle thy handle after thou art donneth.

Thou shalt locketh thy door when taking a dump
for thou shalt never exposeth thy rump.

If thou sprinkles when thou tinkles
thou shalt be neat and wipeth thy seat.

Thou shalt be a good host
For thy guests that thou greet
Stocketh plenty of towels
and fixeth thy damn seat.

Thou shalt not giveth users a filthy towel
Do not leaveth a cloth that's really foul.

When thy hand dryer does not worketh by chance
Thou shalt wipeth thy hands upon thy pants.

Thou shalt not giveth thy host an extra job
Thou shalt wipeth thy seat off, thou lazy slob.

Thou shalt not giveth thy host extra work
Thou shalt wipeth thy seat off, don't acteth a jerk.

Thy bathroom should always be in the pink
Thou shalt cleaneth thy shower, tub, and sink.

Thou shalt clean, clear and scrub
after every use of thy tub.

For Women:

* Useth thy trash can, don't be in a rush
Thy sanitary pads shalt never be flushed.

** If thou has to useth thy pads today
Thou shalt throweth those bloody things away.

*** Thou shalt not forgeteth to throw away thy pads
Thou shalt never maketh thy man be mad.

For Men:

* Thou must treateth women kindly and always lower thy seat
She'll never be angry, as she'll stay dry and neat.

** Thou shalt always remember to putteth thy seat down
Or thy woman just might falleth in and drown.

*** Thou shalt always putteth thy toilet seat down
Or thy woman will greeteth thee with a frown.

Thou shalt never cutteth thy cheese
when thy spouse is catching Zs.

Thou shalt not pee outside in blizzard
Runneth inside and draineth thy lizard.

Thou shalt not crammeth thy toilet, then scram
Flusheth often to preventeth logjam.

Thou shalt not shaketh the hand of thy bathroom neighbor
if thou did not washeth in full after thy labor.

Thy bathroom balance, thou must obey
Closeth thy toilet for proper fêng shui.

Thou shalt not steal thy communion wafer
Neither shalt thou pilfer any toilet paper.

Thou shalt kill no man with stone nor ax
nor thine odor from between thy cracks.

Thou shalt useth thy john for making poopy
Thou shalt not be in there making whoopie.

If thou haveth sex on thy bathroom floor
thou must doeth thy nasty behind locked door.

Thou shalt not covet thy neighbor's wife
Nor his ox, nor his ass
Thou mayest, though, covet thine use of his loo
when thou hast an attack of thy gas.

Against thy neighbor thou shalt not fink
Don't claim it was he who left thy stink
Before thine own odor wafts into thy hall
spray from thy big can of Lysol.

Thou shalt not cloggeth thy toilet drain
unless thou wants to do some plumbing
So be careful what thou putteth down thy commode
or else thou will findeth lots of water coming.

Thou shalt be a good Marine
and taketh good care of thy latrine
Thy movements should remain unseen
so flusheth away thy submarine.

Thou shalt be chided
for urine misguided.

Thou shalt keepeth at hand thy toilet brush
for all those traces that just won't flush.

Thou shalt planneth for fungus defeat
with bathroom slippers upon thy feet.

Thou shalt go to work with freshener spray
when odors threaten to betray.

Thou shalt washeth thy hands post-bidet
or many germs thou shalt convey.

Thou shalt lower thy toilet seat without fail
If not, a mishap may prevail.

Bathroom cleanliness thou shalt not forsake
For it is thy health, thou putteth at stake.

When peeing in the dark
thou shalt taketh careful aim
Be certain of thy bearings
and knoweth thy terrain.

Thou shalt keepeth thy bathroom in good repair
so foul consequences, thou shalt spare.

Thou shalt cleaneth all bathroom taint
prior to any guest's complaint.

Thou shalt not in bathroom bask
Hurry up and completeth thy task.

Thou shalt, upon finishing thy bath
cleaneth thy tub to avoid My wrath.

Bathroom stench thou shalt foresee
and keepeth on hand thy potpourri.

Mildew growth thou shalt impede
or on thy grout, it will proceed.

A clean bath thou shalt not defile
by leaving filth on thy tub or tile.

Thou shalt exit thy latrine
as it was entered, most pristine.

A noisy toilet thou shalt finesse
Thou shalt jiggle thy handle after flushing thy mess.

Thou shalt promptly disinfect
Get rid of thine urine, show some respect.

Thou shalt leaveth no traces behind
upon thy toilet, for others to find.

Thou shalt flusheth thy hopper again and again
until rid of that ungodly stool specimen.

Thy flatulence thou shalt vent
in order to offense prevent.

Thou needeth to showeth good manners now
Locketh thy door before droppeth thy trou.

CHAPTER 3

FARTLETT'S UNFAMILIAR QUOTATIONS

As someone who was quoted in his own time, one would think Confuse-us also enjoyed reading a good quote. There is some evidence to support that he did. He certainly seemed to prior to his split with his former mentor, Confucius.

Confuse-us once said, quite memorably:

> So much to learn, I read all day
> While listening to what Confucius say.

Just a few years later, after he and his mentor split over Confucius's problematic bathroom behavior, Confuse-us's words were much different:

> My master never flush his turds
> So I must now write my own words.

Scholars have debated whether Confuse-us stopped reading Confucius altogether at this point. Did he still follow Confucius's laws outside of bathroom etiquette? Were there other philosophers known to him who helped shape his outlook? We don't know the answer to these questions, but I tend to think that he always enjoyed a good quote.

You may not recognize all of the following quotations in their entirety. Actually, you may not recognize *any* of them in their entirety. But I think you will appreciate where these famous men and women were coming from when they uttered these lines. Well, they certainly *could* have uttered these lines. And they *should* have uttered these lines. That's where my poetic license comes in.

With apologies to *Bartlett's Familiar Quotations* (first compiled by John Bartlett in 1855), think of the following as *Fartlett's Unfamiliar Quotations,* which were not compiled by John Fartlett, but rather by his eminently more distinguished third cousin, Fanny Fartlett. Hey now! So enjoy these fun quotations from the research of Fanny Fartlett, and please heed the wisdom she compiled for us.

When in Rome, poo as the Romans poo.
(with apologies to Pope Clement XIV)

What light from yonder window break?
That shineth down on those who make
If this bathroom guest has offended
Clean it up and all is mended.
(with apologies to William Shakespeare…Romeo and Juliet)

Romeo! Romeo! Where fart thou, Romeo?
(with apologies to William Shakespeare…Romeo & Juliet)

Farting is such foul sorrow.
(with apologies to William Shakespeare…Romeo & Juliet)

Out damn spot. Out I say
My underwear is brown and gray.
(with apologies to William Shakespeare…Macbeth)

When shall we three meet again?
In thunder, lightning or in rain?
Or when the bathroom really smells
and we need to cast our spells?
**(with apologies to William Shakespeare…the Witches
from Macbeth)**

To pee or not to pee?
That is the question.
To pee on the seat?
That's a transgression.
(with apologies to William Shakespeare...Hamlet)

If brevity is the soul of wit
Don't take so long while taking a shit.
(with apologies to William Shakespeare...Hamlet)

Leaving the toilet without pee on the seat
is civilized man's greatest feat.
(Legacy)

It ain't over 'til the fat lady wipes.
(with apologies to Yogi Berra)

I have not yet begun to fart.
(with apologies to John Paul Jones)

Go ahead. Make my bidet.
(with apologies to Clint Eastwood as Dirty Harry)

Tip the canoe, then clean the loo.
(with apologies to President William Henry Harrison)

The only good toilet is a clean toilet.
(with apologies to General Philip Sheridan)

Fart like a buffalo, stink like bee
dump like a donkey and wipe on a tree.
(with apologies to Muhammad Ali)

If you can't stand the stink, get out of the bathroom.
(with apologies to President Harry S. Truman)

The muck's plunged here.
(with apologies to President Harry S. Truman)

There's a crapper born every minute.
(with apologies to P. T. Barnum)

Read my lips. No more flushing lapses.
(with apologies to President George H. W. Bush)

A toilet has nothing to fear, but the rear itself.
(with apologies to President Franklin Delano Roosevelt)

FDR once stood to pee. A pee which will live in infamy!
(with apologies to President Franklin Delano Roosevelt)

Old farts never die. They just fade away.
(with apologies to General Douglas MacArthur)

If at first you don't succeed, flush, flush, again.
(with apologies to Thomas H. Palmer)

Early to drink and early to gush leaves a man ready and willing to flush.
(with apologies to Ben Franklin)

$P=TP^2$ (where P = pee and TP = toilet paper)
(with apologies to Albert Einstein and his theory of relativity)

Don't ask. Don't smell.
(with apologies to President Bill Clinton and his administration)

Man is the only animal who flushes—or needs to.
(with apologies to Mark Twain)

A commode is a potty with a college education.
(with apologies to Mark Twain)

He can't fart and chew gum at the same time.
(with apologies to President Lyndon Johnson)

If a rose is a rose is a rose
then a fart's an affront to your nose.
(with apologies to Gertrude Stein)

Plunging is 1 percent inspiration and 99 percent perspiration.
(with apologies to Thomas Edison)

Flushing isn't everything. It's the only thing.
(with apologies to Vince Lombardi)

George Washington could never tell a lie
He general-ly wiped with extra ply.
(with apologies to President George Washington)

Blessed be they that wipe, for they shall be clean.
(with apologies to Jesus Christ)

Now I lay me down to sleep
I pray the lord, my bathroom to keep
Free of all paper and crud on the floor
'cause cleaning it up is one helluva chore.
(with apologies to the classic eighteenth-century prayer)

One if by land, and two if by sea
Please wash your hands after you pee.
(with apologies to Paul Revere)

Listen my children and you shall hear
of the midnight ride of Paul Revere
He often would stop to take a leak
but he would never stop at privies that reeked.
(with apologies to Henry Wadsworth Longfellow)

'Twas the night before Christmas and all through the house
Not a creature was stirring except one little mouse
Who dropped piles of dung by the chimney with care
You'd best clean 'em up before Santa gets there.
(with apologies to Clement Clark Moore)

Hell no. We won't go.
Unless your toilet's pure as snow.
(with apologies to Vietnam-era protesters)

What happens to a crap deferred?
Does it dry up like a raisin in the bun?
(with apologies to Langston Hughes)

I hope that I will never see
a sloppy misdirected pee
A pee that trails on the floor
a pee that you just can't ignore.

God gave the power to guys like me
to stand up tall and take a pee
And if you miss, won't you agree
to clean it up quite thoroughly.
(with apologies to Joyce Kilmer)

If there's a chicken in every pot
we hope you don't have to crap a lot.
(with apologies to President Herbert Hoover's political opponents)

CHAPTER 4

YINGLES (DON'T BE SKITTISH. IT'S ONLY YIDDISH)

You may not speak Yiddish, but don't worry about it. Even the wise Confuse-us didn't. Of course, he had a good excuse. Yiddish wasn't first used until somewhere around AD 900, almost 1,500 years after Confuse-us was born. And indeed, in his own time, the Chinese language was continuing to evolve. Even today, China has twenty-three provinces, at least seven main dialects and countless subdialects. Even Confuse-us may have gotten a bit confused at times. *Oy!*

Yiddish became an informal, everyday language of European Jews that was a mix of primarily Hebrew (the more formal, book language) and German. As Jews were scattered to various countries, it became a common language that aided communication among them. Jewish immigrants brought Yiddish to America about a century ago, and the language continued to grow.

The beauty of language is that it lives and breathes as it mixes with other cultures. You don't have to know Yiddish to know the following words that have become a part of everyday English: bagel, chutzpah, klutz, lox, schmuck, schtick and many more. As a side note, because Yiddish comes from a variety of languages, you may see these words spelled in different ways. But, well, a bagel and schmear tastes great anytime and anywhere. (If they don't screw it up, that is.)

On a personal note, my maternal grandparents spoke Yiddish in their home, with many colorful daily expressions passed down to my mom of blessed memory. I am happy to say that many of those expressions were passed down to me in the spirit of tradition and love. And the chain continues.

Yiddish also happens to be one of the most fun languages to speak. It's so expressive and colorful! To help you as you read this chapter, I've added a Yiddish Translation Guide at the end of it. And if you don't feel like looking up all the words, just read these Yingles (Yiddish bathroom etiquette jingles) out loud and have a little laugh. In fact, reading this chapter may even prove to be a mechayeh. Just try not to get too farklempt while doing so, okay?

Fulfill your gracious host's fondest wishes
hit the target with all your **pishes**.

If you tend to **pish** all over the floor
some poor **schlemazel** will have quite a chore.

It had been such a long hard day
and I had gotten all **farmisht**
I forgot to lift the toilet lid
and made a huge mess when I **pished**.

When you go to see your physician
and he gives you a bottle to **pish** in
Don't give it back to the man
'til you've wiped all the **pish** off your hand.

Ai-Ai-Ai, Oy-Oy-Oy
Pish in the bowl, you stupid boy!

Don't leave ragged edges
when you rip a sheet
Or the roll will be a **schmatta**
and that's not very neat.

If your guests treat your towels like **schmattas**
and they leave **schmutz** all over your sink
Don't invite those **schnorrers** back
or they might make your toilet stink.

On leaving the john, please quickly survey
now clear all the **schmutz** and disarray.

I did not like what I was smelling
so I sprayed the air, and now I'm **kvelling**.

Clean the bathroom, don't leave it unkempt
Leave the next user feeling **farklempt**.

Do you want to make your parents really **farklempt**?
Clean up after yourself
From this and taxes, you ain't exempt.

Is this bathroom for real or a nightmare I dreamt?
Clean it up, wash your hands and I'll feel **farklempt**.

We interrupt this bathroom program
No, it isn't preempted
To let you know that you're a slob
and we're not feeling **farklempted**.

Time taken cleaning the bathroom
is time that's very well spent
because a sparkling tub and toilet
would make even your mama **farklempt**.

If you don't flush the chair
after poopin' or pissin'
The next bathroom user
will be all **farbissen**.

Why do I always **kvetch** and moan?
You make my bathroom a disaster zone.

Scouring the toilet is no damn fun
So don't be a **kvetch**, just get it done.

"The toilet's stopped up. I'm so **farblunget**!"
Stop your **kvetching**. Just go and plunge it!

Don't leave your little **chotchkes**
a-swimming in the hopper
Flush away those memories
as that would be most proper.

Be a **mensch** and always flush
your **chotchkes** down the drain
Then be a **maven** and grab a brush
and wipe off every stain.

Always rid the bathroom of stain and stench
Be known by all as a perfect **mensch**.

When you shave your face, the sink grows hair
Be a **mensch**, don't leave it there.

Shake your **schmechel** and wipe up the drips
Put the toilet seat down before she flips.

A **schlemiel** leaves crap all over the floor
for the next **schlemazel** who opens the door.

What's the deal, you big **schlemiel**?
You left trash all over my floor
You're a **no-goodnik**, you little **nudnik**
I'm booting you out the door.

Wash your hands right after you wipe
Do not be a **schlemiel**
Or you will spread a billion germs
when you prepare the festive meal.

Don't be a **shmendrik**, don't be a **klutz**
Flush away your crap, you **putz**.

The bathroom's not a synagogue
if you want my opinion
So do your stuff and clean up fast
and don't wait for a **minyan**.

If your bathroom's all **ongepatshket**
please show some class and grace
Clean up the room until you **schvitz**
your work won't go to waste.

It takes a lot of **chutzpah** to leave the bowl unflushed
But that is not a good excuse, not even if you're rushed.

It takes tremendous **chutzpah**
to graze the walls with piss
So always take dead aim, my friend
and never, ever miss.

When crapping in a restaurant
or in a nearby diner
Show a little **sechel**
and sit on a clean liner.

Use a little **sechel**
when you have your business to do
Always wash with liquid soap
and hot water when you're through.

When your boss is trying to pee
that's not the best time to **schmooze**
'cause if he turns his head to see
he might pee on his shoes.

Here I am in the bathroom to make
Believe me, it's better that we do not shake
Nod your head, take a bow
say hi if you choose
but let's wait 'til we're washed up
and outside to **schmooze**.

Don't mess up the toilet seat
Don't be a pariah
Because sitting on a clean toilet seat
is always a **mechayeh**.

What a **mechayeh** to use a bathroom
that's clean and odor free
It's better than even **noshing** on **kugel**
washed down with a cup of tea.

After you flush, don't be a **schnook**
If the water's running, don't just read a book
Jiggle and wiggle the metal hook.

Even when he took a crap
he read his favorite book
Until he dropped it in the john
and clogged it up, the **schnook**.

If you use sturdy toilet paper
that is at least two ply
You'll stand a better chance of
Wiping away all that **chazzerei**.

Wheat bread, white bread, **pumpernickel**, **rye**
Always flush down all your **chazzerei**.

Your host takes great pride in her towels
so don't you treat them like **schlock**
And if you abuse them with grease and grime
she just might clean your clock.

Always make sure to flush down your **peckel**
or you might receive many a heckle.

When you shave, never leave the sink full of stubble
or else, you'll inherit a **peckel** of trouble.

How could you be such a sloppy **schmuck**?
You left such a mess for the next sitting duck.

Someone left the toilet with a great big **schmear**
So it's time to clean it. **Oy vey iz mir**!

When you sit on the potty
make sure your **tuchis** doesn't veer
Or else, you'll be sure
to leave a big **schmear**.

With his **tuchis** wiping, he was best in his sport
There was nary a skidmark in his shorts.

If your **tuchis** needs a spray
use a bidet without delay.

One or two ply, what will it be?
Save your **tuchis** or save a tree?

When you wipe your **tuchis** all clean and shiny
don't let the paper stick to your **heiny**.

Your **heiny** should be paperized
before your gas starts to vaporize.

When wiping up your **tushy**
be aggressive, don't be shy
Never let your toilet paper
be in short supply.

Using toilet paper that's very cushy
can cause dingleberries to hang from your **tushy**.

If your **tushy** isn't firm on the seat
the floor will not stay very neat.

Don't ever let them see your **tush**
even if you're in a rush to flush.

If you get the bum's rush
while sitting on your **tush**
Give the stall door
an extra push.

When you're done with your toilet **schtick**
scour away and do so quick.

Oy vey, just what is this **schtick**?
You're a bathroom **chazzer**. You make me sick!

Flush the toilet when you're all through
or the next in line may scream **Oy gottenyu**!

If you don't want your bathroom to look like a wreck
always make sure to clean up your **dreck**.

Don't leave the bathroom looking like **dreck**
or the **balaboosta** might wring your neck.

If you want your bathroom to be a sparkling haven
get yourself a **balaboosta**, or be a **maven**.

If your bathroom's messy, take some action
or it will become a **tsuris** attraction.

Too much TP in your tidy bowl
will bring you **tsuris** which takes a big toll.

Flush the toilet when you're through
Show some **rachmones** for those after you.

Always tighten the toilet seat bolt
or when you shift, you'll yell **Oy gevalt**!

Oy gevalt! Oh my gosh!
The bathroom's not the place to **nosh**.

If you're in a public restroom
dropping a little **pitseleh**
Make sure the door is closed
so crowds won't stop and *whisteleh*.

When on the toilet he sits and squats
the gas is such, the toilet could **plotz**.

Don't be a **farshtunkenah** by making a big flap
Scour the toilet right after you crap.

When you're scouring your dirty tub
always wear a rubber glove
And when the job is completed
you may shout **Mazel Tov!**

Latkes, kishka, kugel and **knaidel**
Watch where you aim your little **dreidel**.

Mogen David, Manischewitz, Slivovitz and **Schnapps**
Jiggle the toilet handle 'til the water stops.

Clean the shower, really *scrubkes*
Don't leave **bupkis** in the *tubkes*.

Your guests should never have to squirm
Keep them on the friendliest terms
So spread the **nachas**, and not the germs.

Do a **mitzvah** for **mishpucha** and friends
Don't leave bad odors that may offend.

Be a good **boychik**, and show us some class
Spray 'til we're rid of that terrible gas.

Jack be nimble, Jack be quick
Jack cleans the toilet, he's a good **boychik**.

No matter if you're a **boychik** or an **altacocker**
Whether you're a **putz** or a big **k'nocker**
Flush your **dreck** after every movement
And spray the air, for a big improvement.

Don't make your **bubalahs** scream **Oy vey**!
Do your business, **k'nocker**, then flush and spray.

Don't **kibbitz** with strangers
when stopping to piss
You may lose your focus
and the target, you'll miss.

Flush and spray every time
Don't give us a **schpiel**
Those sights and those smells
have zero appeal.

Let your gossipy guests see your bathroom's best
Those **yentas** should come away impressed.

Yiddish-Style Song Parody Titles

1. "The Handy Man"
(to: "The Candy Man"—Sammy Davis Jr.)

2. "Unzippa My Doo-Dah"
(to: "Zip-a-Dee-Doo-Dah"—Disney's Song of the South)

3. "The Schvitz"
(to: "The Twist"—Chubby Checker)

4. "When You Pish Upon the Floor"
(to: "When You Wish Upon a Star"—Disney's Pinocchio)

5. "Too Many Knishes"
(to: "My Favorite Things"—The Sound of Music)

6. "The Dragon Song"
(to: "Puff, the Magic Dragon"—Peter, Paul and Mary)

7. "Don't Get Paper on my Shoes"
(to: "Blue Suede Shoes"—Elvis Presley)

8. "Pish Splash"
(to: "Splish Splash"—Bobby Darin)

TARA SCHUENEMANN

Yiddish-Style Song Parodies

1. "The Handy Man"
(to: "The Candy Man"—Sammy Davis Jr.)

Who can fix the toilet (who can fix the toilet)
when it will not flush? (when it will not flush?)
Plunge the crap all down the drain
and do so in a rush.

The handy man (the handy man)
Oh, the handy man can (the handy man can)
The handy man can 'cause he plunges it with pride
and makes the toilet flush good (the toilet flush good).

Who can make the bathroom (who can make the bathroom)
smell so good and nice? (smell so good and nice?)
When it stinks so badly
that you have to spray it twice.

The handy man (the handy man)
Oh, the handy man can (the handy man can)
The handy man can 'cause he sprays the room with **nachas**
Makes the bathroom smell nice. (the bathroom smell nice)

The handy man brings
every little thing
to make the bathroom smell delicious
Fulfilling all your fondest wishes
He will even flush his **pishes**.

Who can make the bathroom (who can make the bathroom)
smell so good and nice? (smell so good and nice?)
When it stinks so badly
that you have to spray it twice.

The handy man (the handy man)
Oh, the handy man can (the handy man can)
The handy man can 'cause he sprays the room with **nachas**
Makes the bathroom smell nice. (the bathroom smell nice)

2. "Unzippa My Doo-Dah"
(to: "Zip-a-Dee-Doo-Dah"—Disney's Song of the South)

Unzippa my doo-dah. Unzippa dee-ay
My **schlong's** caught in my zipper, **Oy vey**!
Can't you do something? What can I say?
Unzippa my doo-dah, or just go away!

3. "The Schvitz"
(to: "The Twist"—Chubby Checker)

Come on, baby, let's do the **schvitz**
Come on, baby, let's do the **schvitz**
Put a scrub brush in your hand
And go like this.

E-yah, **schvitz**, baby, baby, **schvitz**
Make sure, baby, to use your wrist
Scrub away the **pish**, and do the **schvitz**.

Your guests have all left now
And mama ain't around
Yeah, your guests have all left now
And mama ain't around

We're gonna **schvitz** and **schvitz** and **schvitz** now
Till we wipe it all down.

Come on and **schvitz**
Yeah, baby, **schvitz**
Ooh yeah, and use your wrist.
Come on, don't miss and do the **schvitz**.

E-yah
(Instrumental)

Yeah, you should scrub now where the target was missed
You should scrub now where the target was missed
You really know how to scrub now
You really know how to **schvitz**.

Come on and **schvitz**
Yeah, baby **schvitz**
Ooh yeah
And use your wrist
Come on don't miss, just do the **schvitz**.

('round and 'round and 'round and 'round
Yeah
('round and 'round and 'round, and 'round)
Schvitz right now
('round and 'round and 'round and 'round)
Yeah
('round and 'round and 'round)
Schvitz so good
('round and 'round and 'round)
Schvitz
('round and 'round and 'round)

4. "When You Pish Upon the Floor"
(to: "When You Wish Upon a Star"—Disney's Pinocchio)

When you **pish** upon the floor
you must wipe and clean some more
Don't forget your bathroom chores
it's up to you.

5. "Too Many Knishes"
(to: "My Favorite Things"—The Sound of Music)

Cleaning the toilet bowl, stopped up from **pishes**
and **kugel** and **kreplach**, and too many **knishes**
Matza balls floating, and caca that cling
surely those must be what stopped up the thing.

When it's smelly
when it's stopped up
when I'm feeling sad.

I simply remember I ate all those things
and then I don't feel so bad.

6. "The Dragon Song"
(to: "Puff, the Magic Dragon"—Peter, Paul and Mary)

Puff the magic dragon lives in the sea
with little fish and all their **pish**, and octopuses' pee
Help that magic dragon, that lives in the sea
don't flush any Clorox down, or chemical debris.

7. "Don't Get Paper on my Shoes"
(to: "Blue Suede Shoes"—Elvis Presley)

You need one for the **heiny**
two for the crack
three if you really
have a fart attack
But don't you, mess up my blue suede shoes.

You can crap if you want
but don't mess up my blue suede shoes.

You can crap out loud
have the time of your life
You can even fart
in front of my wife.

Do anything you want to do
but oh no, honey, stay off them shoes.

So don't you
mess up my blue suede shoes
You can crap all you want
but keep paper off my blue suede shoes.

8. "Pish Splash"
(to: "Splish Splash"—Bobby Darin)

Pish splash, I was peeing in the bath
long about a Saturday night
Rub-a-dub-dub, I was splashin' in the tub
thinking everything was all right.

I didn't lock the door
Somebody opened the door
How was I to know there was a party going on?
They saw me **pishin'** and asplashin'…

Yiddish Translation Guide

The following is a guide to the Yiddish words and expressions used in this chapter. Different sources may have multiple spellings for certain Yiddish words. I decided to come up with a system that would make you the most **farmisht.**

Altacocker (Alter Cocker)—An old-timer, sometimes indelicately called an old fart

Balaboosta (Balabusta)—Housewife, homemaker who generally rules the roost quite efficiently

Boychik (Boytshik)—Little boy (said with affection between men)

Bubalah (Bubeleh)—Literally, a baby or little one, but also used as a term of endearment among friends

Bupkis (Bubkes)—Absolutely nothing of value. Less than nothing, really

Chazzer (Chazer)—A pig, generally used to describe a person whose behavior is piggish

Chazzerei (Chazerei)—Junk, garbage, crap

Chotchkes (Tchotchkes)—Playthings, trinkets or decorations

Chutzpah—Gall, nerve

Dreck (Drek)—Dung or feces (literally), or any inferior merchandise

Dreidel—Spinning toy used on Chanukah, or slang for a male organ

Farbissen—Bitter

Farblunget (Farblondzhet)—Aimlessly, cluelessly lost and confused

Farklempt (Verklempt)—Choked up with emotion (epitomized by Mike Myers's old *SNL* "Coffee Talk" character)

Farmisht—Mixed up

Farshtunkenah—Stinky, stinkin'

Heiny (Heinie)—See **Tush(y)**, if you must

Kibbitz—To talk aimlessly, often giving unsolicited advice to others

Kishka (Kishke)—Stuffed derma (sounds delicious, huh?)

Klutz—An exceedingly clumsy person

Knaidel (Knaydl)—Little dumplings found in **matza ball** soup

Knish—A small round or square baked piece of dough often filled with potatoes, liver or kasha

K'nocker—The Big Cheese (or so he/she thinks)

Kreplach—Square or triangular dumplings filled with ground meat or cheese, similar to a ravioli

Kugel—Noodle (or bread) pudding, it's usually good

Kvell—To glow with pride, like a Jewish mama with her son, the doctor

Kvetch—To whine, or it can refer to someone who is a whiner

Latkes—Potato pancakes, traditional fare on Chanukah

Manischewitz—A company known for its sweet wines, **matza balls**, soups and other Jewish culinary necessities

Matza Balls—Balls formed with matza (what else?)

Maven—Connoisseur, expert (can be used derisively)

Mazel Tov—Congratulations! or Good luck!

Mechayeh—Pure joy! Wonderful! Delicious!

Mensch—An honorable guy or gal

Milchik (Milchig)—Dairy products (or food containing milk or cheese)

Minyan—Group of ten men required for public worship

Mishpucha (Mishpocha)—Literally, means family. A close friend can be like **mishpucha** to you

Mitzvah—In common usage, a good deed. So, it's definitely a **mitzvah** to courtesy flush and spray

Mogen David—A famous (infamous is more like it) Jewish wine that is sweet and budget-friendly

Nachas (Naches)—A wonderful feeling of contentment and satisfaction

No-goodnik—Someone always up to no good

Nosh—A little snack, a bite (or, to take a bite)

Nudnik—Pest, nuisance

Ongepatshket—Messy, sloppy, out of order, etc.

Oy Gevalt—Cry of anguish, similar to "Ohmigod!"

Oy Gottenyu—"Oh God!"

Oy Vey (Iz Mir)—A cry of dismay, similar to "Woe is me!" (think Charlie Brown, but in Yiddish)

Peckel (Peckl)—A little bit

Pish—To pee

Pisher—One who pees, or a little squirt

Pishes—What a **pisher** produces

Pitseleh—A wee, tiny bit

Plotz—To burst, or split your guts

Putz—A dolt, a goof

Rachmones—Compassion, mercy

Schlemazel (Shlimazl)—One who perpetually has bad luck

Schlemiel (Shlemiel)—**Schlemazel's** opposite, an inept bungler

Schlock (Shlock)—A piece of junk

Schlong (Shlong)—The male organ

Schmatta (Shmatte)—A rag, or something worthless

Schmear (Shmeer)—To smear, or to *grease* someone

Schmechel (Shmeckel)—The male organ, the Yiddish equivalent to "pecker"

Schmoe (Shmoe)—Your *average Joe*, or often, a rather dull person

Schmooze—To chat (a **Power-schmooze** may connote chatting up the boss in order to curry favor)

Schmuck (Shmuck)—A person with few, if any, redeeming qualities. A dumb **schmuck** usually connotes a sucker

Schmutz (Shmuts)—Dirt, slime, crapola

Schnapps—A strong, dry liquor

Schnook (Shnook)—A meek person, a sucker

Schnorrer—A person who takes but never gives back. A beggar, a bounder, a scrounger

Schpiel (Spiel)—A lengthy, informal monologue usually used to convince someone of something

Schtick (Shtick)—A piece of something, or a comic bit

Schvitz (Shvitz)—To sweat, or to make a big production over

Sechel (Saichel)—Common sense

Shmendrik (Schmendrick)—A dope

Shpilkes—Extreme restlessness, otherwise known as "ants in the pants"

Slivovitz—Plum brandy (favored by some **altacockers**, I am told)

Tsuris—Trouble(s)

Tuchis—Backside, fanny, bottom, butt, **heiny**, etc.

Tush(y)—See **tuchis**; usually referring to an infant's fanny

Yenta—A generally ill-tempered woman who loves to gossip and spread only bad news

REFERENCES

The Joys of Yiddish by Leo Rosten

A Dictionary of Yiddish Slang and Idioms by Fred Kogos

CHAPTER 5

CONFUSE-US–INSPIRED SONG PARODIES (THE LYRICS)

The great Confuse-us enjoyed the music of his era and was said to be an excellent player of the stringed instruments of his time—the guzheng and the pipa. Legend has it that his then-mentor, Confucius, did not like it when Confuse-us would improvise during their jam sessions, as he changed both the melody and the lyrics to their songs.

In an attempt to follow in his musical and lyrical footsteps, here are fifty song parodies written about and for the bathroom, Confuse-us's great area of expertise. As many people restrict their own singing to the bathroom (which is a good thing for all concerned), these parodies seem to be the perfect fit.

You will recognize most, if not all, of the original songs, which span a variety of genres and decades. The parodies will serve as a catchy way of reminding you and others of good bathroom etiquette, and the problems that can ensue when we ignore these rules.

Feel free to sing them anywhere, including but not limited to the shower. Bring them to your next karaoke gathering. Or simply read them as you tap your toes, drop a load, spray the air or do whatever makes you happy. Surely, Confuse-us would approve.

Confuse-us–Inspired Song Parody Titles

The British Bathroom Invasion

1. "Michelle, That Smell"
(to: "Michelle"—the Beatles)

2. "Will You Please Wash Your Hands!"
(to: "I Want to Hold Your Hand"—the Beatles)

3. "You've Got to Flush Your Load Away"
(to: "You've Got to Hide Your Love Away"—the Beatles)

4. "Mother's Little Hopper"
(to: "Mother's Little Helper"—the Rolling Stones)

5. "I Can't Get No Bowel Reaction"
(to: "I Can't Get No Satisfaction"—the Rolling Stones)

6. "Paint It Brown"
(to: "Paint It Black"—the Rolling Stones)

7. "If I Flooded Your Bathroom"
(to: "Tears in Heaven"—Eric Clapton)

Sequels from the Silver Screen

8. "I'm off to Drain My Lizard"
(to: "We're Off to See the Wizard"—*The Wizard of Oz*)

9. "My Rectal Itch Is Bad"
(to: "Ding-Dong! The Witch Is Dead"—*The Wizard of Oz*)

10. "Your Fart Will Go On"
(to: "My Heart Will Go On"—Celine Dion, theme from *Titanic*)

11. "Zippity Spray"
(to: "Zip-A-Dee-Doo-Dah"—Disney's *Song of the South*)

12. "Whistle While You Dump"
(to: "Whistle While You Work"—Disney's *Snow White*)

13. "Yankee Dooted"
(to: "Yankee Doodle"—traditional)

Reruns: TV Show Theme Parodies

14. "A Mess is a Mess"
(to: Mister Ed theme)

15. "Deadly Agent Man"
(to: "Secret Agent Man"—Johnny Rivers)

16. "The Plungers March"
(to: "Mickey Mouse March"—The Mickey Mouse Club theme)

17. "The Beverly Spillbillies"
(to: "The Ballad of Jed Clampett"—The Beverly Hillbillies theme)

18. "A Tale of a Bathroom Slip"
(to: "The Ballad of Gilligan's Island"—Gilligan's Island theme)

19. "The Addams Family Hopper"
(to: "Addams Groove"—The Addams Family theme)

20. "The Grody Bunch"
(to: The Brady Bunch theme)

21. "We Had No Spray"
(to: "Those Were the Days"—All in the Family theme)

Popular Songs Just for Show

22. "Reprehensible"
(to: "Unforgettable"—Nat King Cole)

23. "I Need a Match"
(to: "Matchmaker, Matchmaker"—*Fiddler on the Roof*)

24. "Oh, Sloppy Boy"
(to: "Danny Boy"—Irish traditional)

25. "A Hopper Built for One"
(to: "Daisy Bell (Bicycle Built for Two)"—Nat King Cole)

Unpatriotic and Sacrilegious

26. "The Hymn of the Latrines"
(to: "Marines' Hymn"—the Marine Corps hymn)

27. "Some Poor Bastard's Gonna Sue Ya"
(to: "The Battle Hymn of the Republic (Glory, Glory Hallelujah)"—
American Civil War patriotic song)

28. "When Johnny Cleans Up His Hands Again"
(to: "When Johnny Comes Marching Home"—Civil War–era
patriotic song)

29. "Amazing Crap"
(to: "Amazing Grace"—eighteenth-century hymn)

Country Dumpin' Classics

30. "Maybe I Should've Told You"
(to: "Always on My Mind"—Willie Nelson)

31. "Nasty Gassy Fart"
(to: "Achy Breaky Heart"—Billy Ray Cyrus)

32. "Don't You Make My Blue Bowl Brown"
(to: "Don't It Make My Brown Eyes Blue"—Crystal Gayle)

33. "Butt Gravy"
(to: "Crazy"—Patsy Cline)

That Ole Time Reek and Roll

34. "I Shoot a Stream of Yellow"
(to: "Mellow Yellow"—Donovan)

35. "Reek Around the Clock"
(to: "Rock Around the Clock"—Bill Haley & His Comets)

36. "Poop Dog"
(to: "Hound Dog"—Elvis Presley)

37. "Miss Molly Sure Likes to Dump"
(to: "Good Golly, Miss Molly"—Little Richard)

38. "Bottom of the Bowl"
(to: "Leader of the Pack"—The Shangri-Las)

39. "The Blame Game"
(to: "The Name Game"—Shirley Ellis)

40. "Who Ripped That Nasty Fart?"
(to: "The Book of Love"—The Monotones)

41. "Stinkin' in the Wind"
(to: "Blowin' in the Wind"—Bob Dylan)

42. "You're Just Too Crude to be True"
(to: "Can't Take My Eyes Off You"—Frankie Valli)

43. "The Sound of Flushing"
(to: "The Sound of Silence"—Simon & Garfunkel)

44. "We're Crapping Together"
(to: "Happy Together"—The Turtles)

Classic Reek

45. "Bathroom Man"
(to: "Piano Man"—Billy Joel)

46. "Where There Is Odor, I'll Be There"
(to: "I'll Be There"—The Jackson 5)

47. "I Am Angry"
(to: "I Am Woman"—Helen Reddy)

48. "My, Oh My"
(to: "Hey Hey, My My (Into the Black)"—Neil Young)

49. "Stinkin' Magnolia"
(to: "Sugar Magnolia"—The Grateful Dead)

50. "Y-Don't-U-Spray"
(to: "YMCA"—The Village People)

Confuse-us-Inspired Song Parodies

The British Bathroom Invasion

1. "Michelle, That Smell"
(to: "Michelle"—the Beatles)

Michelle, that smell
is a scent that I know all too well
It stinks like hell.

Michelle, that smell
I don't know how to say this in French
Ooh, what a stench.

I'd love to, I'd love to, I'd love to
Open a window now
and spray the room somehow
And then you'll see that you and me
could sit and breathe well.

Michelle, that smell
I don't know how to say this in French
Ooh, what a stench

I need to, I need to, I need to
I need to leave, you see
This stench is killing me
Until I do, I'm hoping you will know what I mean
I can't breathe…

(instrumental)

I want you, I want you, I want you
To spray the room somehow
You see, I'm dying now
Until I do, I'm hoping you will know what I mean.

Michelle, that smell
I don't know how to say this in French
Ooh, what a stench
And I will spray the room to get rid of this smell I can't stand
My Michelle.

2. "Will You Please Wash Your Hands!"
(to: "I Want to Hold Your Hand"—the Beatles)

Oh yeah I'll, tell you something
I hope you'll understand
After you, use the toilet
Will you please wash your hands!
(2 more times)

Oh please, just for me
I wanna be your man
So please, say to me
You'll really scrub your hands!
(2 more times)

'Cause when I touch you
I feel crappy inside
It's such a feeling that I need
Germicide. Germicide. Germicide.

Yeah you, must do something
I hope you'll understand
After you, use the toilet
Will you please wash your hands!
(2 more times)

'Cause when I touch you
I feel crappy inside
It's such a feeling that I need
Germicide. Germicide. Germicide.

Yeah you, must do something
I hope you'll understand
After you, use the toilet
Will you please wash your hands!
Will you please wash your hands!
Will you please wash your hands!
Will you please wash your hands!!!

3. "You've Got to Flush Your Load Away"
(to: "You've Got to Hide Your Love Away"—the Beatles)

Here I stand with head in hand
I turn my nose to the wall
The turd's not gone, I can't go on
it's stinking up the stall-all-all.

Someone went, I have to vent
my feelings in this way
If I see that messy jerk
He will hear me say-ay-ay.

Hey, you've got to flush your load away
Hey, you've got to flush your load away.

How can I keep my cool
and not make a scene?
Someone went and left a scent
the smell is quite obscene
How could he do this to me
leaving all his turds?
Hey, you clown who left your brown
listen to my words.

Hey, you've got to flush your load away
Hey, you've got to flush your load away.
(Flush, and fade)

4. "Mother's Little Hopper"
(to: "Mother's Little Helper"—The Rolling Stones)

What a drag it is cleaning up…
Things are different today
I see everybody spray
Just to flush is not enough to cleanse the air.

Chorus:
And if you are a good host
You will try to do the most
Make the atmosphere most proper
'Round your mother's little hopper
So your guests will sing your praise
And return without delays.

Things are different today
Sloppy people don't obey
And the fumes of ugly dumps still fill the air.

Chorus:
So people, please
Don't cut the cheese
And if you dump
Please prime the pump
What a drag it is smelling crap.

5. "I Can't Get No Bowel Reaction"
(to: "I Can't Get No Satisfaction"—The Rolling Stones)

I can't get no, satisfaction
I can't get no, bowel reaction
Though I've tried, though I've tried, though I've tried
'Til I've cried
I can't get no
Bowel reaction.

When I'm sitting on my ass
And I'm doing this and I'm doing that
And I just can't pass no gas
And it's like…

Baby, won't you let me, let loose a boom
Can't you see I want to leave this room…
I can't get no
Oh, no, no, no
Hey, hey, hey
I want to dump and spray.

6. "Paint It Brown"
(to: "Paint It Black"—The Rolling Stones)

I see a toilet and I want to paint it brown
That is the color that I most want to drop down
If I sit long enough, until the job is done
I'll have to spray the air, until that smell is gone.

I see a canvas and I want to paint some brown
I want to be the greatest painter in my town
No more will I be standing up to take a pee
I did not foresee this thing happening to me.

I'm on the hopper and I want to make some fudge
Until I get my wish my rump will never budge.

If I sit long enough, I'll start to grimace and frown
I won't be happy 'til I see this bowl is brown
In just a while I will make some Number Two
I did not foresee this thing happening to you.

I'm on the hopper and I want to make some fudge
Until I get my wish my rump will never budge.

I see a toilet and I want to paint it brown
That is the color that I most want to drop down
If I sit long enough, until the job is done
I'll have to spray the air, until that smell is gone.

Doo doo doo doo doo doo doo doo doo doo doo doo oo
Doo doo doo doo doo doo doo doo doo doo doo doo oo

7. "If I Flooded Your Bathroom"
(to: "Tears in Heaven"—Eric Clapton)

Could we still be pals
if I flooded your bathroom?
Would our friendship end
if I flooded your bathroom?

I didn't want
to be so blunt
But my floaters washed ashore
in your bathroom.

Would I be to blame
if I stopped up your toilet?
Would you curse my name
if I stopped up your toilet?

Don't be distressed
I'll clean the mess
'cause I didn't mean to flood
your nice bathroom.

Crap can bring you down
Crap can bring disease
Crap can get me down
Scrubbing on my knees
Let me, please.

(instrumental)

I must confess
It's quite a mess
I sure caused you lots of stress
in your bathroom.

Could we still be pals
if I flooded your bathroom?
Would our friendship end
if I flooded your bathroom?

I didn't want
to be so blunt
But my floaters washed ashore
in your bathroom.

Sequels from the Silver Screen

8. "I'm off to Drain My Lizard"
(to: "We're Off to See the Wizard"—*The Wizard of Oz*)

I'm off to drain my lizard
That fluid-filled lizard of mine
Because I drank a lot of beer
I really must go this time.

My pants are tightening as I speak
I really need to take a leak
Because, because, because, because, because
Because the old bladder is getting weak.
(da, da, da, da, da, da, da, da, da)

I'm off to drain my lizard
That fluid-filled lizard of mine.

9. "My Rectal Itch Is Bad"
(to: "Ding-Dong! The Witch Is Dead"—*The Wizard of Oz*)

Ding-dong, my itch is bad
my wicked itch, my rectal itch
Ding-dong, my rectal itch is bad.

I have a problem here
my rectal itch is most severe
Ding dong, my rectal itch is bad.

I didn't wipe so well
and my butt feels like hell
I must get out of here and change.
('cause)

Ding-dong, my itch is bad
my wicked itch, my rectal itch
Ding-dong, my rectal itch is bad.

10. "Your Fart Will Go On"
(to: "My Heart Will Go On"—Celine Dion, theme from *Titanic*)

Sometimes I'm dreaming
I hear you, I smell you
That's how I know you're still there.

I hear you rip one
I hear it, I smell it
Your gas is still in the air.

Near, far, wherever you are
I believe that your fart will go on
You chose to clog up my nose
And I believe in my heart that
Your fart will go on and on…

11. "Zippity Spray"
(to: "Zip-A-Dee-Doo-Dah"—Disney's *Song of the South*)

Zippity doo-dah, zippity spray
Hey fart-knocker, won't you spray it away?

Plenty of fumes are wafting my way
Zippity doo-dah, zippity spray.

Mister Stinkbomb's in my nostrils
It's the truth, it's actual
The smell is quite unsatisfactual.

Zippity doo-dah, zippity spray
All of your crap is wafting my way.

12. "Whistle While You Dump"
(to: "Whistle While You Work"—Disney's *Snow White*)

Just whistle while you dump
Don't just sit there like a chump
Then make our day and flush away
that ugly brownish lump.

Just sing a happy tune
Don't you gag me with a spoon
Please hum a prayer and spray the air
and leave my bathroom soon.

13. "Yankee Dooted"
(to: "Yankee Doodle"—traditional)

Yankee dooted in the bowl
but did not flush the handle
I went in and smelled the mess
and had to light a candle.

Yankee didn't flush his load
Really left a beauty
Please remember, flush your loads
as you are still on duty.

Reruns: TV Show Theme Parodies

14. "A Mess is a Mess"
(to: Mister Ed theme)

Hello. I'm really mad.

A mess is a mess, oh yes, oh yes
So be sure to clean up your mess, oh yes
Because, oh yes, your messy mess
is messing up my tiles.

So when you're my guest, please do your best
to not make yourself a messy pest
And if you're neat, your host will greet
you with a lovely smile.

People are very sloppy now
and some are really jerks
But you'll never be invited back
if you give them extra work.

A mess is a mess, oh yes, oh yes
I've even left some, I must confess
But your big mess, nevertheless

Well, listen to this
…
I am really mad.

15. "Deadly Agent Man"
(to: "Secret Agent Man"—Johnny Rivers)

There's a man who puts us all in danger
He stinks up the room for every stranger
With every fart he makes
and every dump he takes
odds are we won't breathe until tomorrow.

Chorus:
Deadly Agent Man, Deadly Agent Man
He does his lethal number
and he takes your breath away.

Beware of any fragrances that linger
You never should agree to pull his finger
And if you hear a boom
please scramble from the room
Make sure you can live to see tomorrow.

Chorus

16. "The Plungers March"
(to: "Mickey Mouse March"—The Mickey Mouse Club theme)

Stinky House Plunge
Stinky House Plunge
Stinky House Plunge
Stinky House Plunge

When you have an unflushed turd
that's messing with your brain
P-L-U-N-G-E
Plunge it down the drain.

When you have a piece of crap that's driving you insane
P-L-U-N-G-E
Plunge it down the drain.

Flush your turd
(What's that muck?)
Flush your turd
(What's that muck?)
Forever let us clean the stinking john
John, john, john.

When you have an unflushed turd
that's messing with your brain
P-L-U-N-G-E
Plunge it down the drain.

17. "The Beverly Spillbillies"
(to: "The Ballad of Jed Clampett"—The Beverly Hillbillies theme)

People, listen to a story 'bout a man named Jed
One piss-poor shot who could never hit the head
And then one day he was busy having fun
When out on the floor dropped his big Number One
(Urine, that is. Fool's gold. Texas pee…)

(instrumental)

Now, the first thing you know, old Jethroe had to go
and just like his uncle, he dribbled down below
They said, "Our bathroom is the place you oughtta be
If you cannot hit the pot, and you like to step in pee."
(Fluid, that is. Yellow floors. Sticky shoes.
Y'all be careful now, ya hear?)

(final instrumental)

TARA SCHUENEMANN

18. "A Tale of a Bathroom Slip"
(to: "The Ballad of Gilligan's Island"—Gilligan's Island theme)

Just sit right back and you'll hear a tale
a tale of a bathroom slip
That started from a pissed-on floor
that caused a broken hip.

The culprit was a careless man
the victim grandmama
Two minutes cleaning spent that day
could have saved so much more
Saved so much more.

Grandmama, she's pretty tough
but her walker, it was tossed
He saved two minutes time that day
but her independence lost
her independence lost.

19. "Addams Family Hopper"
(to: "Addams Groove"—The Addams Family theme)

Duh-Duh-Duh-Duh-Fart, Fart
Duh-Duh-Duh-Duh-Fart, Fart
Duh-Duh-Duh-Duh
Duh-Duh-Duh-Duh
Duh-Duh-Duh-Duh-Fart, Fart.

Duh-Duh-Duh-Duh-Fart, Fart
Duh-Duh-Duh-Duh-Fart, Fart
Duh-Duh-Duh-Duh
Duh-Duh-Duh-Duh
Duh-Duh-Duh-Duh-Fart, Fart.

The Addams Family hopper
was smelling very proper
'Til Lurch let loose a plopper
That peeled off the paint.

The walls soon lost their plaster
when Gomez ripped a blaster
It was such a disaster
Morticia had to faint.

Duh-Duh-Duh-Duh-Rump
Duh-Duh-Duh-Duh-Lump
Duh-Duh-Duh-Duh
Duh-Duh-Duh-Duh
Duh-Duh-Duh-Duh-Chump!

When Fester dropped his thunder
the floors soon buckled under
It really is a wonder
they're still alive today.
Fart, Fart

20. "The Grody Bunch"
(to: The Brady Bunch theme)

Here's the story of a sleazy lady
who was bringing up three very sloppy kids
All the girls never flushed just like Mother
who never, ever did.

Here's the story of a man named Grody
who was raising three gross children of his own
They would always stain their trousers just like Father
who never hit the throne.

Then one day when these two sickies got together
he proposed to her while farting during lunch
She accepted his proposal and then pooted
and the two of them soon raised The Grody Bunch.

The Grody Bunch
The Grody Bunch
That's why we call these pigs The Grody Bunch.

21. "We Had No Spray"
(to: "Those Were the Days"—All in the Family theme)

Boy, the way old Grandpa went
Crap that left a toxic scent
Guys like us we had to vent
We had no spray.

And we aired out the whole room
Couldn't borrow Mom's perfume
Mister, we sure could have used some
Piney Clover back then.

When we flushed it down the hatch
after every vile batch
Gee, we had to light a match
We had no spray!

Popular Songs Just for Show

22. "Reprehensible"
(to: "Unforgettable"—Nat King Cole)

Reprehensible, that's what you are
Indefensible, both near and far
You don't flush your droppings down the drain
You leave your napkins showing all your stains
Every damn time, you leave your slime.

Reprehensible, in every way
Indefensible, please go away
But now darling, it's incredible
That your smell's so unforgettable

And you think I'm
Reprehensible, too.

(instrumental)

Reprehensible, in every way
Indefensible, please go away
But now darling, it's incredible
That your smell's so unforgettable

And you think I'm
Reprehensible, too.

23. "I Need a Match"
(to: "Matchmaker, Matchmaker"—*Fiddler on the Roof*)

Matchmaker, Matchmaker, make me a match
Someone just dumped, one nasty batch
I must light a candle to air out the room
so find me the perfect match.

Matchmaker, Matchmaker, what about me?
I have been good, I flushed my pee
But the last user has peeled off some paint
I think that I have to faint.

For God's sake, please get here quickly
For my sake, this room smells like a zoo
But please bring lots of good matches
I can't endure more of this Number Two.

Matchmaker, Matchmaker, make me a match
Someone just dumped, one nasty batch
I must light a candle to air out the throne
So make me a match
of my own.

24. "Oh, Sloppy Boy"
(to: "Danny Boy"—Irish traditional)

Oh, sloppy boy, your crap, your crap is stinking
from room to room, and all throughout the house
We'd like to know, whatever were you thinking
Come back at once, and flush it down, you louse.

So hurry back, you should, you should be rushing
before the house smells like a team of skunks
I will be here, to make sure you are flushing
O sloppy boy, oh sloppy boy, don't be a punk.

25. "A Hopper Built for One"
(to: "Daisy Bell (Bicycle Built for Two)"—Nat King Cole)

Daisy, Daisy, I love you with all my heart
but I'm half crazy, listening to you fart.

I don't have a fancy hopper
but it is only proper.

So please be neat
and wipe the seat
of my toilet, you little tart.

Unpatriotic and Sacrilegious

26. "The Hymn of the Latrines"
(to: "Marines' Hymn"—the Marine Corps hymn)

From the stalls of Montezuma
to the rooms of Tripoli
We have served our country's citizens
on the land and on the sea.

You have dumped your loads inside of us
You must always keep us clean
Don't forget to flush the handle of
your United States latrine.

27. "Some Poor Bastard's Gonna Sue Ya"
(to: "The Battle Hymn of the Republic (Glory, Glory Hallelujah)"—
American Civil War patriotic song)

Glory, glory hallelujah
Some poor bastard's gonna sue ya
He'll be really out to screw ya
if he falls off your seat.

You'd better check to make sure that your toilet seat is tight
If it isn't very sturdy, or it isn't fastened right
When a heavyweight contender sits to poop with all his might
your toilet seat will crash.

Glory, glory hallelujah
Some poor bastard's gonna sue ya
He'll be really out to screw ya
if he falls off your seat.

28. "When Johnny Cleans Up His Hands Again"
(to: "When Johnny Comes Marching Home"
—Civil War–era patriotic song)

When Johnny cleans up his hands again
Hurrah, hurrah
We'll give him a hearty handshake then
Hurrah, hurrah.

He flushed the toilet and left the room
but his hands, he forgot to groom
And we won't shake hands 'til
Johnny cleans up again.

When Johnny stops spreading germs again
Hurrah, hurrah
We'll be on better terms again
Hurrah, hurrah.

His fingers now show a little smudge
Smells like vanilla, but looks like fudge
But we'll shake once more when
Johnny cleans up again.

29. "Amazing Crap"
(to: "Amazing Grace"—eighteenth-century hymn)

Ama-zing Crap
How sweet the sound
So sweet it makes me blush.

I once was bound
But now I'm free
and now it's time to flush.

I stuffed my butt with lots of junk
No fiber could I find
And now I'm stuck upon this chair
It's messing with my mind.

I thought that I might never crap
I was in disbelief
But now that I just pinched a loaf
I'm feeling great relief.

Ama-zing Crap
How sweet the sound
So sweet it makes me blush.

I once was bound
But now I'm free
and now it's time to flush.

Country Dumpin' Classics

30. "Maybe I Should've Told You"
(to: "Always on My Mind"—Willie Nelson)

Maybe I should've told you
I'd been peeing on the throne
And I should've put the seat down
so you wouldn't bitch and moan.

When you sat down on the toilet, dear
and you soaked up your behind
You thought I was so unkind
but you were always on my mind.

Maybe I never told you
that I cried when we were parted
And I guess I never warned you
all ten million times I farted.

Little things I should have said and done
I just never took the time
You thought I was so unkind
but you were always on my mind.

Tell me / Tell me that your sweet smile's not a frown
And give me / Give me one more chance to put the damn lid down
so you'll never drown.

(instrumental)

Little things I should have said and done
I just never took the time
You thought I was so unkind
but you were always on my mind.

You were always on my mind
You were always on my mind.

31. "Nasty Gassy Fart"
(to: "Achy Breaky Heart"—Billy Ray Cyrus)

You might be at home
or sitting all alone
when your heartburn starts to hurt your chest
So what will you do?
The answer's up to you
Rip a big one, and you'll feel your best.

You might be at a meetin'
or hugging on a greetin'
when you feel a rumble down below
Don't fight that simple urge
Go let your bottom purge
Let one loose and really let it blow.

Don't fight your fart, your nasty gassy fart
don't fight it or you'll be in pain
So rip out that big fart, that nasty gassy fart
and you'll stink the air up once again.

(instrumental)

You might be at home
or sitting all alone
when your heartburn starts to hurt your chest
So what will you do?
The answer's up to you
Rip a big one, and you'll feel your best.

You might be at a meetin'
or hugging on a greetin'
when you feel a rumble down below
Don't fight that simple urge
Go let your bottom purge
Let one loose and really let it blow.

Don't fight your fart, your nasty gassy fart
don't fight it or you'll be in pain
So rip out that big fart, that nasty gassy fart
and you'll stink the air up once again.

(instrumental)

Don't fight your fart, your nasty gassy fart
don't fight it or you'll be in pain
So rip out that big fart, that nasty gassy fart
and you'll stink the air up once again.

So don't fight your fart, your nasty gassy fart
or you'll wind up with a fart attack
So rip out that big fart, your nasty gassy fart
as long as I'm not standing at your back.

32. "Don't You Make My Blue Bowl Brown"
(to: "Don't It Make My Brown Eyes Blue"—Crystal Gayle)

Don't know when I've been so down
ever since you came around
Your crap was not flushed down
and don't it make my blue bowl brown.

There's just one thing that I can do
I'll flush your load when you are through
I'll let your crap wash down
'cause I don't want my blue bowl brown.

Tell me no secrets, tell me some lies
Give me no reasons, give me alibis
Tell me you're not such a sloppy guy
Tell me you'll flush or at least you'll try.

Say you'll never leave a mess
Don't leave my john in such distress
You'll let your loads flush down

And don't you make my blue bowl
Don't you make my blue bowl
Don't you make my blue bowl brown.

Don't you make my blue bowl
Don't you make my blue bowl
Don't you make my blue bowl brown.
(repeat last three lines)

33. "Butt Gravy"
(to: "Crazy"—Patsy Cline)

Butt Gravy, why must you give me such heartache?
Butt Gravy, why do you do what you do?
I know, I must wipe you better the next time
Butt Gravy, your brown spots are making me blue.

Hurry, why am I in such a hurry?
Wondering, why did I drop such a poo-oo-oo-oo?
Oh Butt Gravy, my TP could never quite hold you
Butt Gravy, I'm trying, so hard to stop crying
Your brown spots are making me blue.

Butt Gravy, why must you give me such heartache?
Butt Gravy, I'm trying, so hard to stop crying
Your brown spots are making me blue.

That Ole Time Reek and Roll

34. "I Shoot a Stream of Yellow"
(to: "Mellow Yellow"—Donovan)

I'm just mad about bathrooms
Bathrooms are mad about me
I'm-a just-a mad about-a bathrooms, yeah
every time that I have to pee.

I shoot a stream of yellow (Twice nightly)
I shoot a stream of yellow (Twice nightly)
I shoot a stream of yellow (Twice nightly).

When I drink too much fluid
I've gotta stand and take dead aim
When I drink an awful lot of fluid, yeah
target practice becomes my game.

I shoot a stream of yellow (Twice nightly)
I shoot a stream of yellow (Twice nightly)
I shoot a stream of yellow (Twice nightly).

Never takes forever to pee
Getting good night's sleep is nil
Never takes forever to pee
When I want, the bowl I will fill.

I shoot a stream of yellow (Twice nightly)
I shoot a stream of yellow (Twice nightly)
I shoot a stream of yellow
A stream of yellow…

(instrumental)

Eating lots of bananas
will maybe make me feel all right
Eating lots of bananas
I may not have to pee all night.

I shoot a stream of yellow (Twice nightly)
I shoot a stream of yellow (Twice nightly)
I shoot a stream of yellow
Oh so yellow.

35. "Reek Around the Clock"
(to: "Rock Around the Clock"—Bill Haley & His Comets)

One, Two, Three O'Clock, Four O'Clock – Reek
Five, Six, Seven O'Clock, Eight O'Clock – Reek
Nine, Ten, Eleven O'Clock, Twelve O'Clock – Reek
It's gonna reek, around, the clock tonight.

When you use your toilet, night and day
you must spray the room, without delay
Or it will reek around the clock tonight
it's gonna reek, reek, reek, 'til the morning light
It's gonna reek around the clock
less you spray with all your might.

36. "Poop Dog"
(to: "Hound Dog"—Elvis Presley)

You ain't nothin' but a poop dog
a-crappin' all the time
You ain't nothin' but a poop dog
a-crappin' all the time
Well, you never flush the toilet
so you ain't no friend of mine.

Well, you said you had manners
Well, that was just a lie
Yeah, you said you had manners

Well, that was just a lie
Well, you ain't never flushed my toilet
so you ain't no friend of mine.

You ain't nothin' but a poop dog
a-crappin' all the time
You ain't nothin' but a poop dog
a-crappin' all the time
Well, you never flush the toilet
so you ain't no friend of mine.

37. "Miss Molly Sure Likes to Dump"
(to: "Good Golly, Miss Molly"—Little Richard)

Good golly, Miss Molly, sure likes to dump
Wooo, Good golly, Miss Molly, sure likes to dump
She's got me reekin' and a-rollin'
can't she flush away that lump?

From the early-early mornin'
'til the hurly-burly night
She don't give me no warnin'
she just spoils my appetite.

Good golly, Miss Molly, sure likes to dump
She's got me reekin' and a-rollin'
can't she please control her rump?

38. "Bottom of the Bowl"
(to: "Leader of the Pack"—The Shangri-Las)

He never flushed his waste
He went out of his way to put the seat up
You get the picture
(Backup Singers: Yes, we see)
That's when I fell to the bottom of the bowl.

(sounds of flushing)

He'd always pig out and get the runs
(runs! runs!)
Unload a ton of crap from his buns
(unload his crap from his buns)
He never flushed in my palace
He put the seat up with malice
That's why I fell to the bottom of the bowl.

(sounds of flushing)

I felt so helpless what could I do?
(do! do!)
My legs were wet and covered with poo
(were wet and covered with poo)
He put the seat up, that fool
Now my butt's covered with stool
That's why I fell to the bottom of the bowl.

(sounds of flushing)

39. "The Blame Game"
(to: "The Name Game"—Shirley Ellis)

The blame game…

Shirley!
Shirley, Shirley, Bo-Birley
Won't you act more girly?
If you fart, you're leaving early
Shirley.

Lincoln!
Lincoln, Lincoln, Bo-binkin
Once again, you're stinkin'
My oxygen is shrinkin'
Lincoln.

Come on everybody
I say, let's play a game
First one who cuts the cheese
takes all the blame
So, please have a heart
and don't cut a nasty fart.

(more song instructions)

Herman!
Herman, Herman, Bo-Berman
Bo-nana-Fana, Fo-Ferman
Did you cut the cheese, you vermin?
Herman.

My game is very easy and it works every time
Because farting at a party is a brutal crime.

(more song instructions)

Everybody do Bucky!
Bucky, Bucky, Bo-Bucky
You won't be very lucky
if you step on that ducky
Bucky.

Pretty good, let's do Tommy!
Tommy, Tommy, Bo-Bommy
Bo-nana-Fana, Fo-Fommy
Don't cut the salami
Tommy.

Very good, let's do Doris!
Doris, Doris, Bo-Boris
Bo-nana-Fana, Fo-Foris
We don't want to hear that chorus
Doris.

A little trick with Nick!
Nick, Nick, Bo-Bick
Bo-nana-Fana, Fo-Fick
Your fart's making me sick
Nick.

The blame game...

40. "Who Ripped That Nasty Fart?"
(to: "The Book of Love"—The Monotones)

I wonder, wonder, wonder, wonder who (fart sound)
Who ripped that nasty fart?
Mama, mama, mama
I love you with all my heart
Please don't tell me baby that
you ripped that smelly fart.

Well, I wonder, wonder, wonder, wonder who (fart sound)
Who ripped that nasty fart?

Mama, mama, mama
You wouldn't do that to me
I'm sure you wouldn't leave me here
in utter misery.

Well, I wonder, wonder, wonder, wonder who (fart sound)
Who ripped that nasty fart?

One, you should confess now
and make amends to us
Two, you better leave the room
and run and run and run to the porcelain bus
Three, you must remember
to use your head and think
That you must spray some fragrance
When your load really stinks.

Well, I wonder, wonder, wonder, wonder who (fart sound)
Who ripped that nasty fart?

Mama, mama, mama
I love you with all my heart
Please don't tell me baby that
you ripped that smelly fart.

Well, I wonder, wonder, wonder, wonder who (fart sound)
Who ripped that nasty fart?

One, you should confess now
and make amends to us
Two, you better leave the room
and run and run and run to the porcelain bus
Three, you must remember
to use your head and think
That you must spray some fragrance
When your load really stinks.

Well, I wonder, wonder, wonder, wonder who (fart sound)
Who ripped that nasty fart?
Mama, mama, mama
I love you with all my heart
Please don't tell me baby that
you ripped that smelly fart.

Well, I wonder, wonder, wonder, wonder who (fart sound)
Who ripped that nasty fart?
I, wonder who...yeah
Who ripped that nasty fart?

41. "Stinkin' in the Wind"
(to: "Blowin' in the Wind"—Bob Dylan)

How many times must a man move his bowels
when his whole system is stuffed?
Yes, and how many times must a man flush his chair
after unloading his duff?

Yes, and how many times must a man spray the air
before he has sprayed it enough?
The answer, my friend, is stinkin' in the wind
The answer is stinkin' in the wind.

42. "You're Just Too Crude to be True"
(to: "Can't Take My Eyes Off You"—Frankie Valli)

You're just too crude to be true
Can't take my eyes off of you
You'd be like heavens to touch
if you did not crap so much.

And I just don't understand
why you never wash your hands
You're just too crude to be true
Can't bear to stay here with you.

Pardon the way that I sneeze
whenever you cut the cheese
You know, the air really reeks
My breath is getting quite weak.

So, please know how I feel
I'm just keeping it real
You're just too crude to be true
Can't take my eyes off of you.

(instrumental)

I love you, baby
But if it's quite alright
I need you, baby
to not cut cheese tonight
I love you, baby
Don't get mad when I spray.

Oh, stinky baby
Be good to me, I pray
Oh, stinky baby
I just ran out of spray
And let me breathe some fresh air
Won't you, baby?

You're just too crude to be true
Can't take my eyes off of you
You'd be like heavens to touch
if you did not crap so much.
And I just don't understand
why you never wash your hands
You're just too crude to be true
Can't bear to stay here with you.

(Instrumental)

I love you, baby
But if it's quite all right
I need you, baby
to not cut cheese tonight
I love you, baby
Don't get mad when I spray.

Oh, stinky baby
Be good to me, I pray
Oh, stinky baby
I just ran out of spray
Oh, stinky baby
Trust in me when I spray.

Oh, stinky baby (fade)

43. "The Sound of Flushing"
(to: "The Sound of Silence"—Simon & Garfunkel)

Hello toilet, my good friend
I've come to squat on you again
Because the baked beans that I just woofed down
had me churning out some lumps of brown.

And the droppings that are clogging
up your drain will not remain
After the sound of flushing.

All through the night, I crap alone
while I talk on my cell phone
In the bathroom in the early morn
all my toilet paper's now been torn
I've been sitting, squeezing loads with all my might
a gruesome sight
Before the sound of flushing.

TARA SCHUENEMANN

44. "We're Crapping Together"
(to: "Happy Together"—The Turtles)

Imagine me and you, I do
I think about us every time, I'm on the chair
I think about us stinking up, the bathroom air
We're crapping together.

If I could buy another bathroom chair
then you could join me and unload your derriere
Imagine how the two of us, could spoil the air
We're crapping together.

I could never be with nobody but you
for all my loads
When you're with me, baby the bowls will be blue
in our commodes.

Me and you, and you and me
No matter how we drop our loads, it has to be
The only crap that you will see, will come from me
We're crapping together.

I could never be with nobody but you
for all my loads
When you're with me, baby the bowls will be blue
in our commodes.

Me and you, and you and me
No matter how we drop our loads, it has to be
The only crap that you will see, will come from me
We're crapping together.

(ba, ba, ba, ba Chorus)

Me and you, and you and me
No matter how we drop our loads, it has to be
The only crap that you will see, will come from me
We're crapping together.

No matter the weather (ba, ba, ba, ba)
We're crapping together (ba, ba, ba, ba)
We're crapping together (ba, ba, ba, ba)
(repeatedly)

Classic Reek

45. "Bathroom Man"
(to: "Piano Man"—Billy Joel)

It's ten o'clock on a Saturday
The regular crowd is all there
There's an old man sitting next to me
who left skidmarks in his underwear.

He says, "Son, can I share a quick memory?
I'm not really sure how it goes
But I once was quite neat and I even smelled sweet
when I wore a cleaner man's clothes."

Oh, la, la-la, di-di-da
La-la di-di-da da-dum

Give us advice, you're the bathroom man
Show us the way today
'cause we're all in such need of a remedy
and you help us feel okay.

Now, Tom at the bar never flushes
whether he poops or he pees
And he has a good heart, but he's quick with a fart
and he wears lots of cheap dungarees.

He says, "Larry, my habits are killing me"
but a grin now spreads over his face
"I can't keep a job or a girlfriend
I'll soon be kicked out of my place."
Oh, la, la-la, di-di-da
La-la di-di-da da-dum

Now, Paul never wipes off the toilet
and he leaves all that mess for his wife
And he's speaking with Davy
who still has butt gravy
And probably will have for life.

Yes, the whole bar has gross hygiene habits
as they swap all their stories of gloom
And they're sharing a lifetime of messiness
but they're happy to share the same room.

(piano fill)

Give us advice, you're the bathroom man
Show us the way today
'Cause we're all in such need of a remedy
and you help us feel okay.

It's still a good crowd for a Saturday
and the manager shoots me a smile
'cause he knows I'm the man who always flushes the can
and even will scrub off the tiles.

And the bathroom soon smells like a garden
and the toilet like fresh potpourri
And they heed my advice and they even look nice
and say, "Dude, you're much cleaner than me."

Oh, la, la-la, di-di-da
La-la di-di-da da-dum

Give us advice, you're the bathroom man
Show us the way today
'cause we're all in such need of a remedy
and you help us feel okay.

46. "Where There Is Odor, I'll Be There"
(to: "I'll Be There"—The Jackson 5)

You and I must make a pact
We must bring good hygiene back
'cause there is odor everywhere.

I will flush the chair for you
if you spray away your poo
Where there is odor, I'll be there.

And oh, I'll be there to comfort you
Spray a gentle breeze around you, I'm so glad that I found you
I'll be there with a glove that's strong
I'll even scrub, I'll keep scrubbing on (yes, I will).

Let me spray the room from floor to rafter
A pleasant smell, well that's all I'm after
Whenever the room stinks, I'll be there.

I'll be there to inspect you,
with a bottle of spray to protect you
Where there is odor, I'll be there.

And oh, I'll be there to comfort you
Spray a gentle breeze around you, I'm so glad that I found you
I'll be there with a glove that's strong
I'll even scrub, I'll keep scrubbing on (yes, I will).

If your room should ever smell like poo
I know that this should never happen to you
But if there's odor, I'll be there.

Don't you know baby, yeah yeah
I'll be there, I'll be there
Where there is odor, I'll be there.

Just cover your nostrils, honey. Ooh

I'll be there, I'll be there
Where there is odor, I'll be there.

47. "I Am Angry"
(to: "I Am Woman"—Helen Reddy)

I am woman, hear me roar
There is something you ignored
You did not put the seat down once again
You must think this is a joke
that I got my butt all soaked
And that's the reason that I hate all men.

Oh yes, I am wet
But I can see through the pain
I will wring your neck
if you do this again
If I have to, I can do anything
You are wrong (wrong)
You are despicable (despicable)
I am angry.

You can soak but never break me
As your heartlessness will make me
more determined to achieve all of my goals
You are weak and I am stronger
and you won't be here much longer
If you ever make me fall into the bowl.

Oh yes, I am wet
But I can see through the pain
I will wring your neck
if you do this again
If I have to, I can do anything
You are wrong (wrong)
You are despicable (despicable)
I am angry.

48. "My, Oh My"
(to: "Hey Hey, My My (Into the Black)"—Neil Young)

Hey hey, my my
Spray the air or I might die
Please don't treat my bathroom
like your own pig sty
Hey hey, my oh my.

Way too much brown came out of your back
I'm suffering from your sneak attack
And once you crap, you can't come back
When way too much brown comes out of your back.

Your crap's now gone but it's not forgotten
I've never smelled something quite so rotten
It's better to spray now so I can sleep
Your crap is gone but it's not forgotten.

Hey hey, my my
Spray the air or I might die
Please don't treat my bathroom
like your own pig sty
Hey hey, my oh my.

49. "Stinkin' Magnolia"
(to: "Sugar Magnolia"—The Grateful Dead)

Stinkin' Magnolia, butt is booming
She breaks wind, and I don't care
Smelled my baby down by the river
Knew I had to take in some fresh air.

Sweet little blaster under my pillow
We can have good times if you'll abide
We can discover the wonders of hygiene
If you spray the bottle and use some germicide.

She's a wonder in my kitchen
She can really cut the cheese
Opens the window when I get a headache
Says "God bless you" when I sneeze.

(Instrumental)

She's a very classy lady
She always thinks of fun things to do
But she's just a little bit gassy
Just a little gassy between me and you.

She can cook a five-course meal
She makes me happy that I'm alive
But she spoils the air in the spring, fall and summer
And when it's crappy, I need to revive.

Stinkin' magnolia
I'm holding a bottle
Caught up in sunlight
Come on out spraying
I'll walk you in the fresh air
Come on baby, walk along with me.

She's a wonder in my kitchen
She can really cut the cheese
Opens the window when I get a headache
Says "God bless you" when I sneeze.

Sometimes when my baby's sleeping
Sometimes when the smells abound
Sometimes when my breath is dying

I take me out and I spray around
I spray around.

Sweet, sweet daydream
Walking through the fresh air
Avoiding where the wind goes
Blowing into my nose.

Breathing more freely
Nights spent spraying
I'll walk you in the morning fresh air
Fresh air daydream
Walk you in the fresh air.

50. "Y-Don't-U-Spray"
(to: "YMCA"—The Village People)

Young Man, stop your lazing around
I said Young Man, don't just sit there and frown
You can help out when your load is flushed down
There's no need to be unhappy.

Young Man, do you know what I think?
I mean Young Man, this whole room really stinks
You can help us get this room in the pink
It should not be smelling crappy.
doo-doo-doo-doo-doo...

It's fun to flush but then
Y-Don't-U-Spray?
It's fun to flush but then
Y-Don't-U-Spray-ay?
You can take any smell that was left in the air
You can spray the room everywhere.

It's fun to flush, but then
Y-Don't-U-Spray?
It's fun to flush but then
Y-Don't-U-Spray-ay?
You can get the room clean, be all proud of yourself
The spray is right on the shelf.

Young Man, won't you heed all my words?
I said Young Man, now that you've flushed your turds
But the smell in here is simply absurd
Spray the room and we'll be happy.

Young Man, I'm so sick of this smell
I mean Young Man, this room still stinks like hell
You should treat it like a fancy hotel
It should not be smelling crappy.
doo-doo-doo-doo-doo...

It's fun to flush but then
Y-Don't-U-Spray?
It's fun to flush but then
Y-Don't-U-Spray-ay?
You can take any smell that was left in the air
You can spray the room everywhere.

It's fun to flush, but then
Y-Don't-U-Spray?
It's fun to flush but then
Y-Don't-U-Spray-ay?
You can get the room clean, be all proud of yourself
The spray is right on the shelf.

CHAPTER 6

BATHROOM ETIQUETTE NURSERY RHYMES AND SING-ALONGS

Confuse-us believed fervently in being a good role model for children, including his own three kids. The bathroom scholar once wrote:

> Children should explore and play
> But bathroom rules they must obey
> So easy to flush and use the spray

Indeed, he was all about teaching kids from an early age to be considerate to their family, friends and neighbors. Legend has it that Confuse-us put the following teaching to music, so kids could sing along while learning proper bathroom behavior:

> Bring to others satisfaction
> Be considerate in words and action.

Quite a few centuries later, the first popular nursery rhymes were written in the English language. Frankly, some popular nursery rhymes are a little bizarre, yet they are memorable and somewhat musical. They remind me of bad debts or bathroom odors: they tend to stay with us for a long time. That said, some of you may have your own favorite nursery rhymes, and after reading this chapter, you may now see them in a brand new light.

Sing-Alongs

"Crappy Birthday to You"
(to: "Happy Birthday to You")

Crappy birthday to you
Go have fun in the loo
I have cleaned up the toilet
so it's ready for you.

We don't mind if you do
Take a swell Number Two
Just as long as you clean up
for the ones after you.

"Treat All Bathrooms Carefully"
(to: "The ABC Song")

A-B-C-D-E-F-G
Treat all bathrooms carefully
H-I-J-K-L and M
Don't you leave bad smells in them
N-O-P-Q-R-S-T
Throw away all your debris
U-V-W-X-Y and Z
Keep it clean for you and me.

Nursery Rhymes

Little Miss Muffet, sat on a tuffet
doing her daily duty
Then along came a spider
who sat down beside her
What she left just wasn't too cutey.

Little Miss Muffet sat on a tuffet
needing to make Number Two
Along came a spider
who died right beside her
'cause she didn't spray scent in the loo.

Hey diddle diddle, your kid made a piddle
right next to the toilet floor
Your host will not laugh
to see such a gaffe
And you won't be invited no more.

Eeny meeny, miny, moe
Caught the toilet tissue on your toe
Who was inconsiderate?
That bum who chose to litter it.

Little Betty Blue could not make a poo
before she ate up some prunes
So, Little Betty Blue returned to the loo
and barked out some happy tunes.

Humpty Dumpty sat on the throne
He placed a toilet guard down
since it wasn't his own
All the king's horsemen found the used *Charmin*
and what happened to Humpty was more than alarmin'.

Humpty Dumpty sat on the throne
Humpty Dumpty sighed a great moan
He rolled off the pot
and on the rug left a spot
that couldn't be removed
not a little, nor a lot.

Jack be nimble, Jack be quick
Jack jumped into the bathroom because he was sick
He later recovered from the explosive attack
but when his host saw the bathroom
he couldn't come back.

Old MacDonald had a tub—E-I-E-I-O
And on that tub, he used to scrub—E-I-E-I-O
With a rub, rub, here, and a scrub dub there
Here a rub there a scrub
Everywhere a tub scrub
Old MacDonald had a tub
Now he can bathe there without fear.

One, two, clean up the loo
Three, four, discard junk from the floor
Five through eight, don't hesitate
to erase all trace when you urinate.

There was an old woman who lived in a shoe
She never took care of her things, or her loo
Don't let this scenario happen to you
So clean up your bathroom—you know what to do.

Hickory, Dickory, Dock
to the bathroom, we do flock
The clock strikes two
We're happy to poo
Now clean up 'fore someone doth knock.

Wee Willie Winkie runs through the town
upstairs and downstairs though his bladder is sound
Tapping at the windows, crying all around
Do you have a clean bathroom
or a breeding ground?

Old King Cole was a merry old soul
And a merry old soul, as he sat on his bowl
But he was dismayed when he saw the bidet
had been littered with tissue in complete disarray.

Sprinkle tinkle on the hopper
clean it up and make it proper
Soap and water, first apply
then you wipe to make it dry
If your tinkle goes awry
make pristine or folks will cry.

Tinkle, tinkle, little man
hit the target as you planned
Poised above the bowl to hose
pick your spot and down it goes
Tinkle, tinkle, little man
now it's time to flush the can.

Jack and Jill went up the hill
to use a little outhouse
Down Jack squat
but he missed the pot
and poor Jill cleaned up after.

Simple Simon met a pieman
going to the fair
Said the pie man to Simple Simon
There are no bathrooms there
Said Simple Simon to the pieman

Man, what did you do?
I pulled down my pants and took a chance
and doo-doo'd in my shoe.

Pins and needles, needles and pins
when I miss my target, my troubles begin.

There was an old man who loved to eat beans
He ate nothing else, not even his greens
Now you might think this was a strange diet
That's why this old man could never be quiet.

Little Bo Poop got lost from his group
and went in the woods to find them
He looked for his map while taking a crap
and left quite a trail behind him.

Mary, Mary, quite contrary
how does your garden grow?
With lots of water and lots of sunshine
and all of my crap in a row.

If all the world were apple pie
and all the seas were ink
And all I ever ate were beans
this world would really stink.

CHAPTER 7

FOR WOMEN ONLY

Ladies, this chapter was not easy to write. We are well aware that yours is the neater, lovelier, and more verbal gender. No debate: Men take the silver medal in all these categories.

Now, given that I am in awe of your proficiencies in each of these categories, allow me to speak my mind. I must ask you… What is going on behind those closed bathroom doors? Hey, I don't mean this in a personal or perverted way. It's just that we never want to see any evidence that you were in the bathroom. We just want to admire that beautiful, refreshed, clean-shaven, indefinable you. So, please keep us in mind.

Other bathroom users have the right *not* to see the following items in clear view: sanitary pads (especially unwrapped ones), diapers, excessive makeup on sinks and counters, and any articles of clothing. And please use your best judgment in what you flush down the hopper.

As the happily married Confuse-us once said:

> Woman who shows used sanitary pad
> Makes even the calmest man go mad.

I think Confuse-us would want you to keep the following friendly bathroom etiquette tips in mind.

Please refrain from flushing sanitary pads
They really stuff the toilet bad
When all this crud backs up the thing
It's like a horror novel by Steven King.

When you get the monthly menace
your work's cut out for you
Lay in supplies like Motrin and pads
and just survive the moods
But where does it say that when hormones flare
we should lose self-respect?
Wrap your napkins and dispose of them
We have reputations to protect.

Every month you expect
to have a visit from your friends
So now you should prepare yourself
with Tampax and Depends
Each of these convenient items
has a disposable part to chuck
And ladies, if you are sloppy
the next girl's out of luck.

Regarding your all-used tampons and strings
Your soiled maxi-pad with absorbent wings
Your condoms, your Kotex, your diaphragm rings
Don't you dare flush them down the damn thing.

Ladies, pleases follow our advice
We'll try to say this very nice
If you need to use your pads today
Please throw those bloody things away.

When your monthly friend pays a visit
don't be in such a dash
that you forget to deposit
your soiled pads in the trash.

Have pity on the bathroom maid
who follows you, poor wench
For you have left your blood-soaked pads
in addition to the stench.

My gosh! Yeegads!
Don't flush your sanitary pads.

As a polite lady, after you've dined
you may now need to relieve your behind
In a proper manner, nice and refined
You must carefully flush to be kind.

Women, is your makeup on your face, or on the sink?
Do you ever wonder who looks great in pink?
The lipstick and the blush look good on you
But clean up the basin when you're through.

Do you shave your pits and thighs
to look your best for all the guys?
Maximize your attraction
then take some cleanup action.

Pretty is as pretty does
or so the proverb goes
Crumpled TP and messy pads
create a ton of woes.

Round and round Queen Victoria ran
'til she found Prince Albert alone in the can
If such a thing should happen to you
don't bother your prince, until he is through.

A disposable diaper chucked in the can
will foul up the breathing of the bravest man.

CHAPTER 8

FOR MEN, THOUGHTFUL OF WOMEN

Okay, it's time to address my own gender. Ladies, feel free to read along. I think I've represented your concerns well.

Here's the deal. There are way too many divorces in this country. If you're not an attorney, I'm sure you'll agree. Hey now!

Frankly, increasing marital harmony is one of my goals for this book. To that end, I researched the main causes of domestic disputes: infidelity, poor communication, jealousy, economic hardship, and unshared responsibilities. These are all important causes of domestic disputes, but the number one cause (you may not be surprised) is…men not lowering the toilet seat after taking a leak. I don't know all the reasons that an unreturned toilet seat freaks women out, but it just does. So be respectful of that concern!

The wise Confuse-us, in no uncertain terms, spoke on this very issue:

> Man who never returns seat to the throne
> Will find himself often sleeping alone.

With this wisdom in mind, unless you are in a bathroom that is used *only* by men, never leave the toilet seat up after doing Number One. And, if you intentionally leave the toilet seat up after doing Number Two (just to be a troll), you are one bad guy!

A flush of the hopper leaves it most proper
The lowered seat makes the job complete.

To err is human
to forgive divine
But to leave the seat up
is an unspeakable crime.

Don't leave in a rush
right after you flush
If the seat's not put down
the next user might drown.

Do not offend your lady friend
right after you pee
Put the seat down right away
for domestic harmony.

In a restroom, the gender gap is wide
If he leaves the seat up, she likely falls inside.

She casually lowers her derriere
most shockingly, she plunges there
To not lower the seat was a man's decision
that puts her now in an awkward position.

Respect the appearance of your partner's anus
Leaving the seat up is conduct most heinous.

If you open the door that says *Men*
and find one of the fair sex within
Apologize first and do not stare
Wait 'til she gets her butt outta there.

CHAPTER 9

A BREATH OF FRESH AIR

This has most likely happened to you. Nature is calling, and it's an emergency call. Finding the bathroom quickly becomes priorities number one and number two, if you know what I mean. As you find the bathroom, you're starting to feel good about life again.

Then, you open the door, and…phew! The aroma wafting from the privy almost knocks you flat on your back. You are temporarily paralyzed. Evidently, some inconsiderate, crap-happy user just produced a stench that singes your nose hair and causes your eyes to tear. This deadly gas has even started to peel the paint off the bathroom walls.

We're talking a Level 10 stench on the Reek-ter Scale, which, as you may know, was developed by the late great Swedish scientist, U. R. Reeking. Hey now! So now, what do you do? Search for another bathroom, which may be as foul-smelling as the first? Or do you tough it out by holding your breath, taking a dump, cleaning up and moving out ASAP?

This is the classic dumper's dilemma. Stay and suffer through this nasal Armageddon, or go and risk not finding another john, or finding one in equally dire straits.

I usually react to this dilemma by flipping a coin—outside the bathroom, of course, where I can actually breathe. I won't lie to you. It's simply a dreadful situation to be in. All because of some louse who dumped and ran!

Do not be like that louse. Do not dump and run, without courtesy flushing, flipping on a vent fan, spraying the room, or opening a window afterward. Please remember that a courtesy flush is a quick flush after dumping and prior to wiping.

You must use this stench-reducing measure as a courtesy to all those who use the facilities after you. If you have courtesy flushed and there is no spray, vent fan or window available to you, that is the best you can do in this situation. In this case, the person responsible for the bathroom needs to get their act together.

Always strive to be like the wise Confuse-us who eloquently wrote:

> Man who sits and craps a ton
> Must flush and spray when he is done.

> No one knows a scent so foul
> as when a man lets loose his bowels
> What should he do when the deed is done?
> Spray the john and quickly run.

> Go until your abdomen's hollow
> But in stench you must not wallow
> Come on dude, please be a gent
> Deodorize that putrid scent.

> You sit on the john bent over double
> thinking "Dear God, am I in trouble"
> I ate like the devil and I'm cramping like hell
> Oh Lord, deliver me from this smell.

> If you're on the toilet and smell your own bowels
> now's the time to be wise as an owl
> The smell's enough now to make you howl
> so spray away that smell most foul.

When you leave the royal throne
don't keep that smell entrenched
Use the spray to freshen the air
and rid us of that stench.

Always be aware and show that you care
Give the next user a breath of fresh air.

It always makes me mad
when the bathroom smells so bad
If it's you who made the fume
please be kind and spray the room.

We still await the shrewd inventor
of the automatic smell de-scenter
But until then, friends, let's clean and spray
Without us, the odor will stink and stay.

Enter the bathroom and stop right there
What is that God-awful smell in the air?
If you opened the window and spray was used
your nostrils wouldn't feel so abused.

When taking a poop
the air he would taint
The smell was so bad
it would peel the paint.

There is a toxic yet colorless fume
escaping from your powder room
So close the door and flip on the fan
whenever you choose to use the can.

When nature is calling
and the scent is appalling
It's okay to use the spray
Now all the odors will go away.

You sit on the throne and read your paper
around you wafts a disturbing vapor
Flip to the want ads to answer your prayer
Desperately seeking "a breath of fresh air."

If you poot when you doot
the point is not moot
Be thoughtful today
and give it a spray.

Always be kind to your fellow man
Spray the room after you use the can.

Most wisely, a gent
engages the vent
He knows not to fail
or try to turn tail.

The fumes were so bad
when on the toilet he'd sit
we'd always make certain
a candle was lit.

Please leave the bathroom in the pink
Spray the air and kill that stink.

The bathroom should smell like a bed of roses
Protect the olfactory nerve in our noses.

When stink bombs explode
down the old commode
Open the window, and please don't wait
and you won't have to fumigate.

Aim the spray throughout the bathroom
Good riddance to foul air
Freshen up your living space
with fragrant savoir faire.

If you're going to crap and fart
please don't tear my bathroom apart.

All eyes would tear, the weak would faint
when in the toilet he left his taint.

Much worse than an onion
that made my eyes tear
were the fumes that unfurled
from his nasty rear.

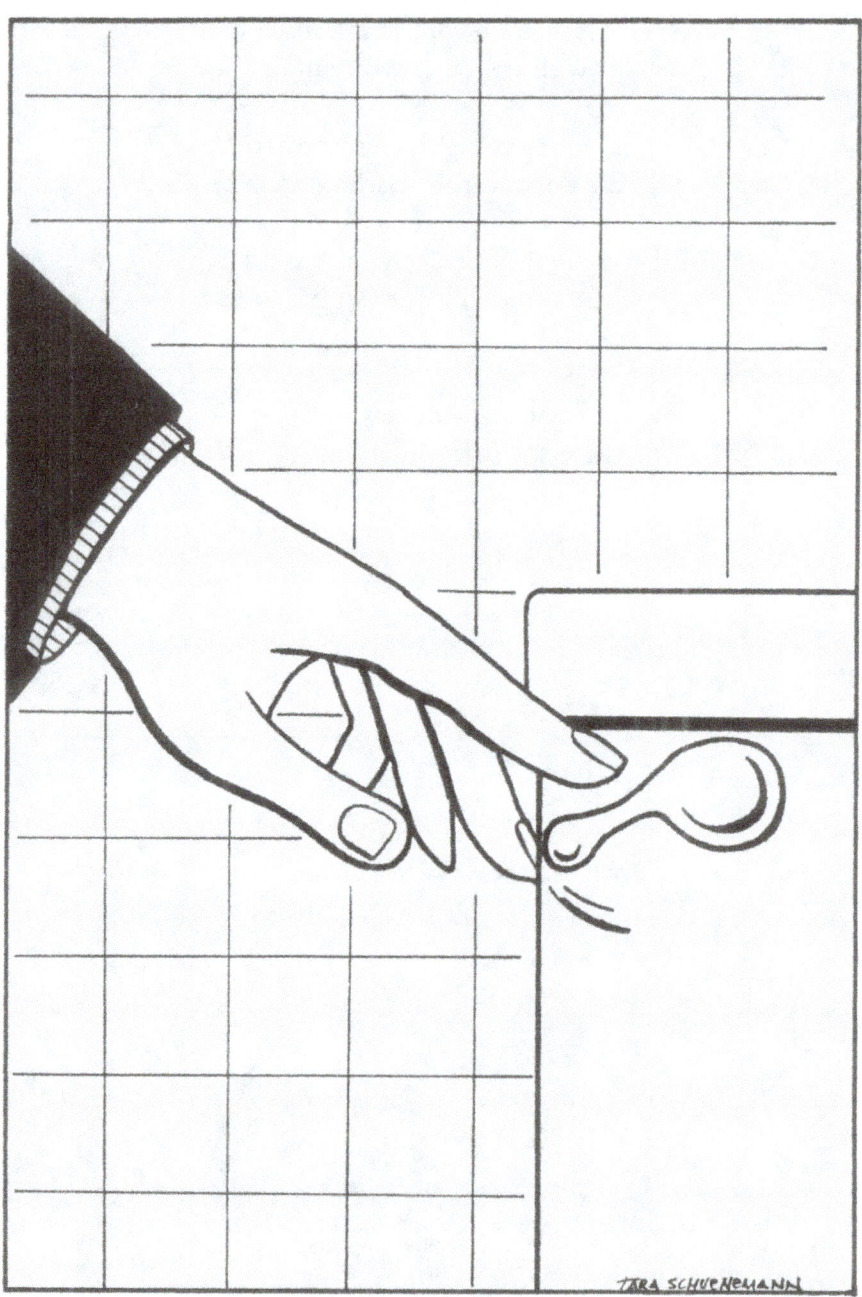

CHAPTER 10

FLUSH NOW OR BLUSH LATER

Nature is calling you. Perhaps she is texting or DM'ing you. Or even BM'ing you. Hey now!

No matter what, this is an emergency. You need to answer the call and board the porcelain bus before you are doubled over in pain. You've reached your destination and you're ready to dump, but lo and behold, you are greeted by an unflushed bowel movement. This brownish log seems to be looking up and taunting you. Oh, disgraceful humanity!

How could someone be so disgustingly thoughtless? What kind of barnyard animal would leave the hopper in such a deplorable state? As your anger slowly subsides, you realize that there are only three explanations for this antisocial behavior:

#1 This slob made no attempt, whatsoever, to flush the toilet. Totally inexcusable!

#2 That mystery log-cutter tried to flush but didn't stick around to check on the toilet's progress. It's not quite as bad as the first case, but still unpardonable.

#3 This hapless crapper tried their best, but the toilet didn't have enough suction to complete its mission. The flesh was willing, but the porcelain was weak. They are excused if they employ other measures.

So what should *you* do when you encounter the leftover log from hell, and the toilet just won't flush? Remember that you must not risk tweak-

159

ing a clogged john. This can turn a somewhat harmless log into an over-flowing submarine. You must use a plunger, if one is available, or you must notify the person in charge of the bathroom. You'll be glad you did.

Always flush the toilet, and never flush and run without checking to see if the flush was completed. You have failed if you don't plunge the bowl when a plunger is readily available. It is also a failure to not notify the responsible party when the toilet cannot be flushed. If you are the responsible party, it is your duty to repair any toilet that is incapable of flushing a power-dump. You also must provide plungers and maintain (or replace, if need be) your porcelain facilities at all times.

Take it from Confuse-us, who evidently felt very strongly about this issue:

> Folks need to flush, and leave no traces
> Or they should never show their faces
> They'll never be in our good graces.

> Keep your bowel movements a mystery
> Flush them down 'til they're history.

> Some people ball toilet paper up
> while others fold it neatly
> No matter which way you prefer
> please flush it down completely.

> Remember that seeing is believing
> Flush thoroughly when done relieving.

> When you pinch a loaf that weighs a pound
> don't let your loaf just loaf around
> Flush that brown bread down the drain
> We don't want to see that loaf again.

> If you want to make sure your host isn't moody
> be a good guest and flush your doody.

Flush all your movements
right down the drain
Save the next user
both odor and pain.

If what you left would make you blush
be a pal and give it a flush.

If your bowels start to rumble
and out of you the contents tumble
don't leave that gruesome stench right there
flush that oh so precious chair.

Some make deposits in the bank
All make deposits in the tank
In the bank, your interest makes cash grow
Flush the tank, as the interest is low.

If you gaze in the toilet
and spot some brown
be a good sport
and flush it down.

If in the loo, there's an auburn hue
that some jerk left as residue
flush again and return to white
as brown is not a pleasant sight.

As you sit and bask in the reek
while on the kingly throne
Give the hopper a courtesy flush
Don't make the rest of us groan.

Don't be an inconsiderate oaf
Flush down that gross, unsightly loaf.

Only the most uncaring fool
would not flush down that nasty stool.

Extra, extra, here's the latest scoop
Don't make headlines, just flush your poop.

Leaving your excrement on public display
is looked upon in a nasty way.

This basic little bathroom ditty
addresses a subject that's not too pretty
Whatever you leave in this, our privy
should not make others faint or dizzy.

Ah, the blissful anticipation
when you suffer from constipation
If prayers and medicine offer releases
clean up after your party ceases.

When you flush the toilet
make sure it goes down
Your brownish surprises
will make someone frown.

His pose on the commode
made him appear like *The Thinker*
His failure to flush
revealed him the stinker.

When you brew up that big load
make sure it goes down the commode.

Consider the toilet's point of view
When the user takes a poo
it is not something it wants to savor
So flush completely as a favor.

When running to the bathroom
with a frantic urge to pee
if you find a clogged-up toilet
that's a real tragedy.

Please keep this bathroom from being stinky
You may even be a little kinky
Flush the toilet and use your pinky.

When you finish peeing in the potty
and you notice the water is yellow
flush the tank and don't be snotty
be kind to the next-in-line fellow.

Remember, right after your big deposit
flush everything down the water closet.

Cut down on the paper
and be a smart shopper
Don't flush a whole roll
down your trusty old hopper.

Don't use too much TP
before you flush
or the pipes will be jammed
and the water will gush.

When you flush at thirty thousand feet high
all your crap is released in the sky
Aren't you glad that you won't be around
when it lands on some poor slob on the ground?

If you've just used a liner to keep your butt clean
Flush that liner down the latrine.

Toilet paper by the wad
can cause a lot of damage, by God
While your bottom may feel fresh and clean
your plumbing bills may become obscene.

My toilet water's like a swimming pool
So please be cool
and flush your stool.

The bathroom's not an art museum
Don't let people see your BM.

If the toilet's stopped up from your stool
the plunger is a handy tool.

If you keep the john clean with a cleaning brush
you have good intentions so please don't rush
Don't you dare forget to flush.

CHAPTER 11

A TIME AND A PLACE FOR EVERYTHING

I enjoy a firm handshake or respectful fist bump in addition to the occasional reassuring pat on the back. Who doesn't? From time to time, a hearty embrace gives me that warm-and-fuzzy feeling that carries me through the day. Having said that, I also realize there is a time and a place for everything.

I don't want the guy who just walked away from the urinal, whether zipped or unzipped, extending one of his filthy paws for me to clasp. It can wait, I'm sure. And I especially don't relish a warm-and-fuzzy from the dude who just power-dumped in stall number three, even if he is a long-lost friend, cousin or coworker.

There are even some misguided people out there who refuse to give you the time of day out on the street, but if they spot you in the john, they're suddenly running for president. They want to shake your hand, even as they case the room for babies to kiss. This is deplorable conduct, to say nothing of the bathroom user who runs out the door without even washing his or her hands. Unthinkable!

So, please don't follow in these hygiene abusers' footsteps or handprints. Heed the instructions of the great bathroom scholar Confuse-us, who once warned:

> Always follow my bathroom laws
> Don't shake hands with dirty paws
> Exposing germs and human flaws.

Don't rush to make contact after you dump
Especially if you've dropped a large lump
Now's not the time for a hearty hand pump
Scrub off your mitts and we'll do a fist bump.

If you've just used the toilet
you'll have to understand
that nobody wants to shake
your unwashed, filthy hand.

Greetings in the bathroom
will not come off as planned
unless you make the effort
to scrub your outstretched hand.

I was washing my hands after using the facilities
when a guy I knew offered his gratuities
He was still in the john and wanted to shake
but I thought it improper right after you make.

If you run into a long-lost friend
and your bowel movement comes to an end
Don't greet them 'til you wash your hands
I'm sure that they will understand.

I'm thrilled to meet you but please understand
I don't want to shake your disgusting hand.

You gotta go when you gotta go
But even so, despite the time demands
don't forget to wash your hands.

One small prayer, seldom voiced
on hands shaken, slightly moist
I hope he did, he knows he ought
to wash his hands as his mother taught.

Did you ever wonder
if the person who was just seated
washed their hands before they sat down
or if they cheated?
All of the microbes
and all the germs they still wear
might as well be invited
and offered a chair.

Every time you have to go
please remember what you know
Wash your hands and wipe the sink
I mean, what would your mother think?

A regular purge, your doctor will urge
A wash of the hand is the public demand.

Scrubbing your hands with soap and friction
Strengthens your case against slander and fiction.

After you're done whizzing
make sure you wash up
Get rid of those germs
or become a sick pup.

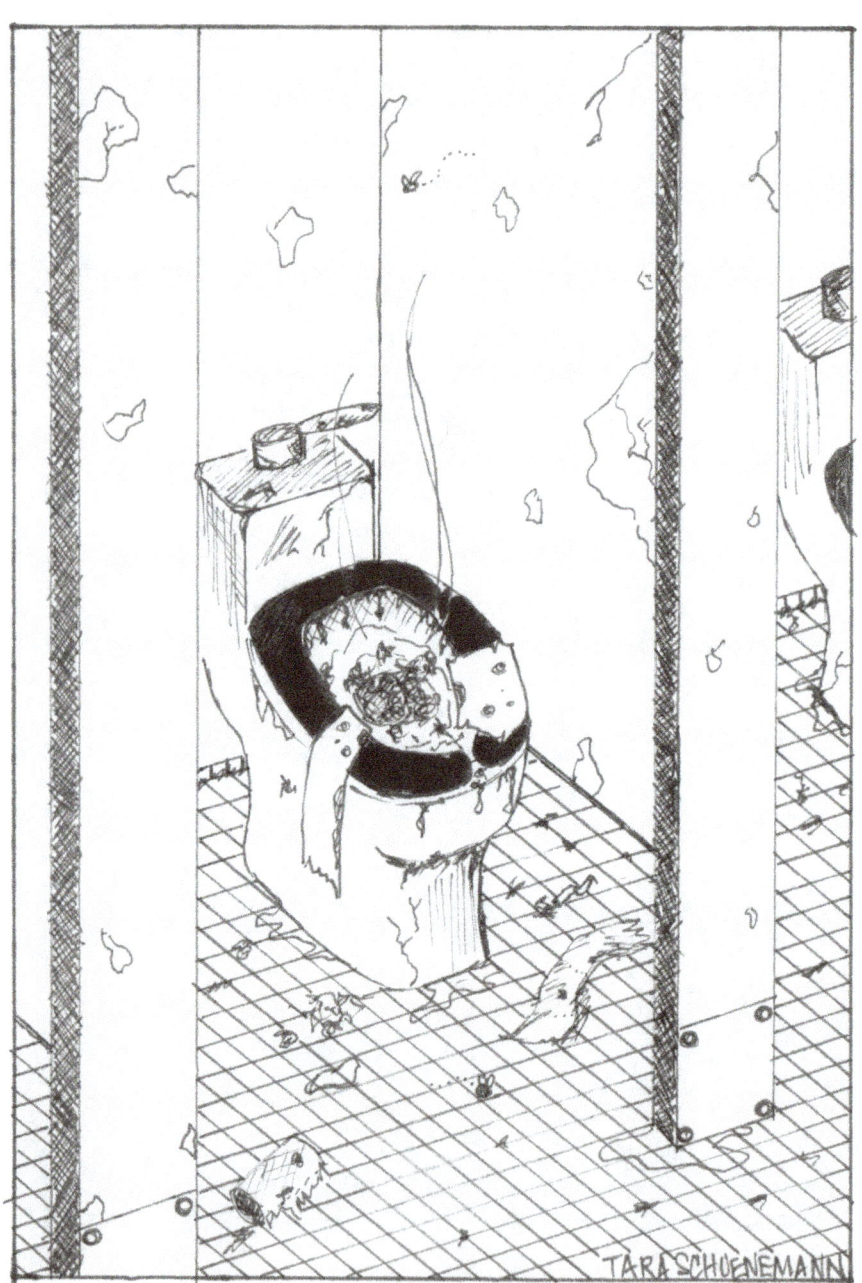

CHAPTER 12

CLEANLINESS AND THOUGHTFULNESS ARE NEXT TO GODLINESS

As a person of refined taste, you appreciate cleanliness and thoughtfulness. They sure beat messiness and thoughtlessness, don't they? Especially in the bathroom, where there is vast potential for messiness and thoughtlessness.

How many times have you looked forward to a soothing, relieving bathroom experience only to have it ruined by the disgusting condition of the room? Perhaps the floor, or the toilet seat, is swimming in urine or covered with caca. Maybe you have encountered used seat liners, or strips of soggy toilet paper clinging to the seat or bowl. Or maybe you arrived to find the sink and counter covered with some combination of soap, makeup, toothpaste, water and hair. Not very appetizing, and certainly not conducive to dumping a good load!

We are often forced to waste valuable minutes cleaning up after others who were simply thoughtless in their actions. Mostly because they were just too lazy and inconsiderate to clean up properly after themselves. The result of their messiness and thoughtlessness is often an ungodly mess that we must face.

We need to be considerate to one another at all times, and in all places. The great Confuse-us recognized the need to thoroughly clean the toilet seat, rim, and, if necessary, anywhere else needed, including its under-carriage, after we finish our business.

Little-known fact: Confuse-us wrote specifically about this oft-neglected part of the toilet:

> Man will have unhappy marriage
> If he doesn't clean the undercarriage.

Confuse-us also warned us to dispose of all used toilet seat liners, and to not leave any evidence of toilet paper on the floor. He cautioned us not to neglect the counter and sink, and to never *decorate* it with soap, makeup, hair, toothpaste, or anything else that will spoil the ambience for the next user. So, please, honor his example. Remember to curb your ungodly behavior and practice cleanliness and thoughtfulness at all times.

> If you sprinkle when you tinkle
> please be neat, use a sheet and then wipe the seat.

> When you need to pee
> but misdirect your wee
> don't make someone quibble
> Just clean up your dribble.

> Lift the lid or pee through the middle
> 'cause it isn't any fun sitting in your piddle.

> Toilet seat liners should be used
> but they should not be abused
> You must always be discreet
> Don't leave used liners on the seat.

> Totally unsuspecting, you enter the stall
> The toilet is littered and you are appalled
> The last patron papered, to keep their butt clean
> To have left the used paper is downright obscene.

When you cover the toilet seat in neat little squares
do you think that the next guest is even prepared
for the sight of your artwork
strewn on floor and on seat?
So clean up behind you
Give the next user a treat.

Make sure you line the potty seat
but leave no paper when done your feat.

Make sure to groom the hopper
upon a dirty toilet seat
But make sure that your fanny
doesn't stick to a single sheet.

When you sit on this, our potty
please don't leave it wet and spotty
Clean it 'til you see your reflection
That way, no one gets an infection.

Target set and take your shot
Oh my God, you missed the pot!
Maybe next time you'll improve your aim?
Not! Wipe up the drips and a bull's eye you'll claim.

Don't take a leak while standing in the dark
for if you do, you may miss your mark.

Be sure to clean the toilet rim
The offerings there can look mighty grim.

Bathroom visits become less sweet
when someone messes up the seat
Believe you me, it's quite a job
to clean up after the average slob.

When you use a public restroom
it's still a private thing
If you clean up for your neighbor
he will think himself a king.

If you are wondering why the bathroom
is so important to us
We spend so many intimate moments there
It's worth a great big fuss.

When you were first potty trained
your mother left you with the reins
She hoped that when she closed the door
you would not pee on the floor.

Make sure your backside doesn't budge
Don't adorn the floor with messy fudge.

When you take a dump
never leave a smudge
So make sure your rump
doesn't even budge.

When you're finished doing your Number One
put the seat down when you're done.

Perhaps a maid would appear and erase
your ugly bathroom sloppy trace
But she does not exist, my friend
and I have found your crime
Now I have to clean it up
and waste my precious time.

Do not engage in gross deceit
Wipe thoroughly the toilet seat.

THE LEGEND OF CONFUSE-US

To chance upon a tainted loo
is a terrible sorrow
In your grief, you'll find no relief
perhaps until tomorrow.

The smallest task, I did forget
a deed undone, as of yet
A spot so small, just barely wet
But oh the trouble it did beget
a painful impact I sorely regret.

If you splash standing tall in the pot
and the seat becomes stained with your spot
It is clear that you mis-aimed your shot
Blot the pot and don't say, "I forgot!"

Hey guys, it's not very hip
to let your wet old weenie drip
Always shake off your final drops
after your stream of yellow stops.

When you go to the head while you're out at sea
Make sure you swab right after you pee.

Please be a sweetie
and clean up the toilet seatie.

It doesn't matter if the colors match well
if the guests leave the bathroom looking like hell
The matching towels and fancy rug
won't camouflage that creeping crud.

Once this sink was clean and dry
Now it's you who has to try
Wipe it off for your good host
Don't be labeled a guest who's gross.

From just one basin defiled
many a man becomes reviled.

Please excuse me if I stare
but the sink is full of hair
And there is a certain scariness
that you did not clean this hairiness.

Toothpaste and soap all over the place
getting so bad you can't see your face
Just imagine how you could look
if you would wipe off all that gook.

When you squeeze the toothpaste, don't be hasty
For if you are, the sink will get pasty.

Toothpaste left in the sink
really makes you think
that each multicolored blob
was left by a careless slob.

CHAPTER 13

ADDRESSING ISSUES OF TOWELS AND TISSUES

There are tons of issues that concern us every day, such as paying our bills, feeding our family, and getting along with our neighbors. Also, there are a variety of issues that concern us every day in the bathroom, including the burning issues of how to use towels and toilet tissues.

Think about it. Have you ever just moved your bowels (not very far, but they did reach your destination… Hey now!) only to discover that you did not have enough toilet paper to complete your wipe? Or, for that matter, any toilet paper to even start to wipe?! Sadly, we've all been there.

Did you ever follow some oaf leaving a public restroom only to find that this inconsiderate jerk used way more toilet paper than necessary, leaving you with a paltry quarter inch of one ply to get the job done? I'm livid just thinking about it. I could go on and on about the misuse of toilet paper, but I'll spare you my wrath for now.

There are also many mistakes made with bathroom towels. Have you ever had guests ignore the paper towels or small guest towels you set aside for their use, choosing instead to rub their greasy mitts all over your premium bath towels—and you don't even realize it until it's too late? Or perhaps your guests use the paper towels, but they leave them all over the floor.

Remember always to use bathroom towels and toilet paper responsibly. Take care not to commit any of these violations: ignoring the guest towels and messing up the host's premium towels; tearing toilet paper unevenly, ruining the roll for the next user; or intentionally rolling toilet paper under, while visiting a household of over-rollers, or vice versa. Good guests respect their hosts' wishes on such matters.

Confuse-us expounded at length on this last issue, saying:
In my home, I always roll it over
When my host prefers to roll it under
If I change their way, they'll react with thunder
So, my fellow guests, don't commit this blunder.

Confuse-us, a generous bathroom host, took pains as a guest to never use more toilet paper than he needed, so the next users would always have enough for their own needs.

Let me add another note of caution about the proper use of towels and toilet tissues:

When using TP in a public restroom, make sure you don't emerge from the john with toilet tissue hanging from your shoes. Although this may not be a classic violation of noble bathroom conduct, it is not a very chic look. I have taken a few steps in public with TP on my shoes, and no one even had the courtesy to tell me. They just snickered a bit, just as I do when I am the observer. Remember, there are always a few sneaks out there ready for you to make a fool of yourself for their entertainment. Don't give us (I mean *them*) any ammunition.

Please don't soil the fancy towels
or you won't be welcome to move your bowels.

If you are in a powder room
which is lavishly adorned
don't use the fancy guest towels
or by your hostess you'll be scorned.

If your greasy mitts stain the fancy towel
your host will greet you with a scowl.

Every time you feel the spirit
brewing in your bowels
Enjoy the pleasures of a dump
then wash and use the towels.

If you see a paper napkin
for the guests to use
Don't soil the fancy, costly one
the two shouldn't be confused.

As you sit and ponder world issues
and clean up with your toilet tissues
Don't let the tissues stick to your shoes
as that will make you front page news.

Toilet paper always feels great
and keeps one's backside happy
But toilet paper on one's shoe
makes you look extremely crappy.

Leaving the john in a hurry
is not the best thing to do
'cause someone may be laughing
at the TP on your shoe.

If you walk out in public with TP on your shoes
you may soon be singing those *Sloppy Walkin' Blues*.

Before that business meeting
where you're the featured speaker
Please remove the toilet paper
off your shoe or sneaker.

Don't leave me stranded on this poop chair
Have a heart and leave more than a square.

That moron used all the paper
I have quite the gripe
Wait 'til I get my messy hands
all over that asswipe.

A jerk who was always unfair
was wiping his butt on the chair
Though he had a fresh roll
he damn near used it all
and didn't leave even a square.

When you've finished wiping, please take care
and give the TP a nice clean tear.

Make sure you tear your toilet paper on the perforated line
or else your roll will look like a wild growing vine.

The toilet roll, she would end with a fold
making it easy for all to take hold.

When using your host's toilet paper
don't commit this blunder
If your hosts like to like roll it over
never roll it under.

When you replace your toilet paper
on that little roller pin
Make sure to slide it on top down
and give it the right spin.

People from all over the world
no matter which flag they've unfurled
Love to ponder burning issues
such as which way to roll their toilet tissues.

If you use the men's room there in the mall
and you find no tissue within
Just ask the fellow in the next stall
"Ya got two fives for a ten?"

Use toilet paper freely
when you have diarrhea
Using just a single ply
is not a great idea.

When you have visitors to your latrine
give them toilet paper that's soft and clean
So treat your fine guests like kings and queens
provide cushy ripples in blues and greens.

Quilted toilet paper removes the unsightly
while treating your bottom most politely.

If you wipe up with a quilted sheet
your butt will be on Easy Street.

Toilet tissue that's soft with quilt
allows firm wiping without much guilt.

On toilet paper that's finely grooved
wiping action is much improved.

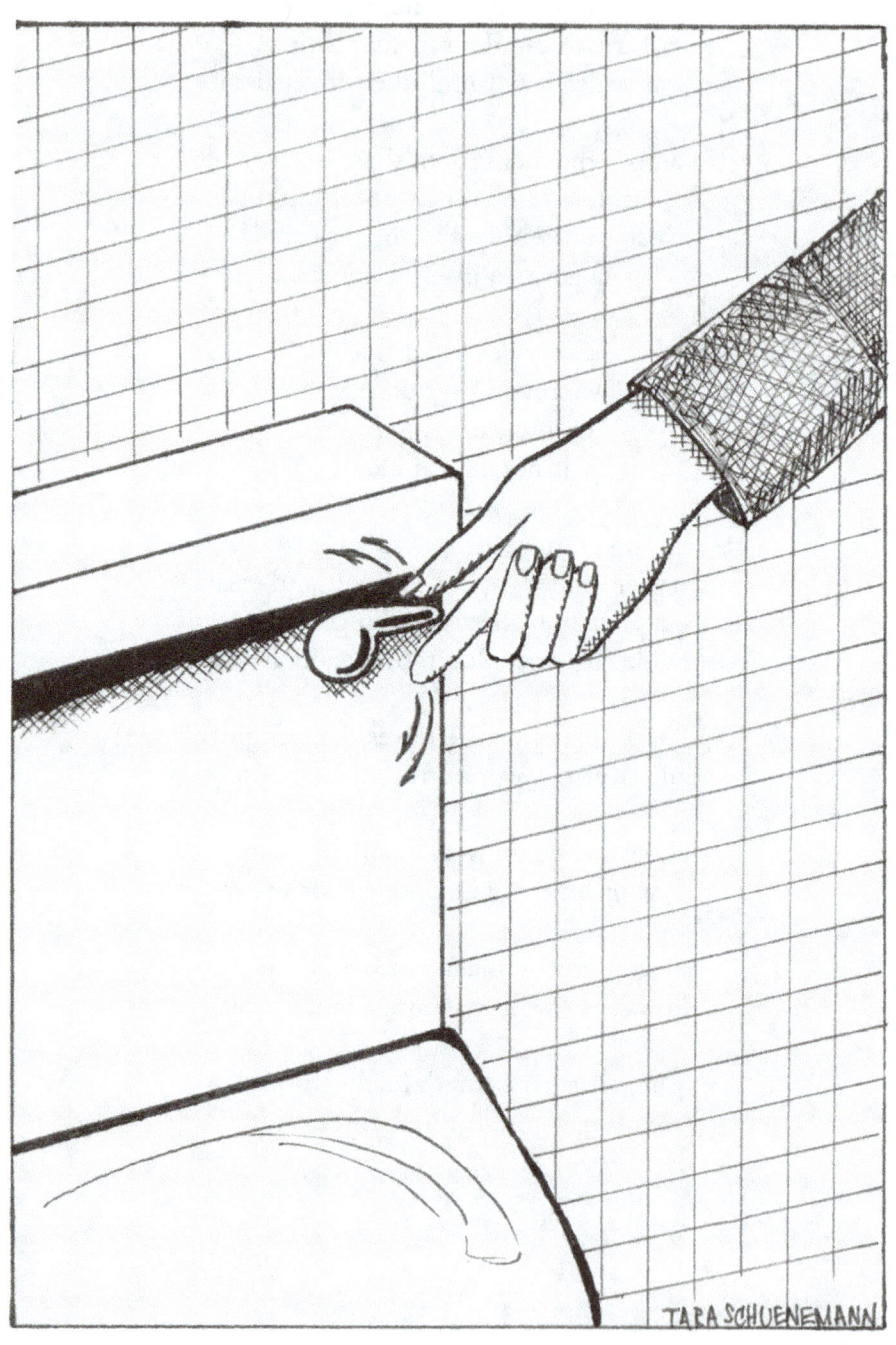

CHAPTER 14

GIVE IT A JIGGLE, GIVE IT A WIGGLE

It's time to talk about a very serious bathroom issue. The problem of the running toilet. You just don't want it to run, and run, and run, and... You get the idea. Your toilet shouldn't be running the marathon after it's flushed. Yet occasionally your toilet, like you, gets the runs. So what do you do?

Simply give the handle an extra jiggle, and the problem is alleviated 99 percent of the time. Hey, nothing's foolproof. But the jiggle demands so little time and effort. Just turn your wrist a little now and save yourself a lot of problems in the future.

The great Confuse-us actually wrote a rare nonrhyming teaching about this very issue:

> Ping-Pong player has magical wrist
> But what good is this great attribute
> If it isn't used to stop a running toilet?

As Confuse-us was married to a professional Ping-Pong player, we don't know if this teaching was directed specifically to his wife. I would say that it was directed to each one of us.

The ever-running toilet, apparently, drove Confuse-us to distraction, as it has done to all of us. It's noisy, to say the least, and it's not a very soothing sound. Nobody wants to go to sleep with the sounds of a wheezing, sneezing, hissing, pissing, slab of ceramic within earshot. A noisy, running hopper can wake you up in the middle of a pleasant dream and even destroy your fragile psyche during the waking hours. To say nothing of potential overflows and high water bills. Yes, that noisy, running hopper is not only a major nuisance, but it also has the power to make the sanest of us go berserk. This is no exaggeration.

Here is the lesson: If you are responsible for a noisy, running toilet and do not have it repaired, you are at fault, and worthy of criticism. Even if you are only using the facilities and hear the ever-running toilet and choose to ignore it, you, too, are negligent.

Dear readers, please make an effort to cut down on the amount of running toilets out there in our bathrooms. In the process, you will greatly reduce noise pollution and sleep deprivation, and also cut down on the number of people suddenly raging for no apparent reason. After you've completed your flush, don't rest on your laurels. If you hear that the toilet is still running, be an instant hero and give the handle a jiggle. If need be, give it a wiggle, too. Make Confuse-us proud.

Spend the extra time it takes
to best complete your flushing
Jiggle the handle as need be
to stop the water's rushing.

Don't leave the toilet running on
because you're feeling lazy
Jiggle the handle 'til it stops
or it will drive you crazy.

Make sure the toilet stops running
when the flusher is released
Or it may keep running all night long
disturbing your family's peace.

Jiggle the hook after you flush
if you consider yourself wise
Then your toilet won't keep running
and your water bill won't rise.

After you flush the toilet
don't just run away
The handle may need a jiggle
so the water won't run all day.

Jiggle the handle after you flush
Please don't leave in such a rush
This kind action saves us all
from a potential waterfall.

Jiggle the handle when you're done
It would really help a ton
I guess we could find a plumber to call
But just jiggle and we won't need him at all.

If your movement leaves a nasty smell
you may need to light a candle
If your toilet keeps running after the flush
you need to jiggle the handle.

After your flush is over
please take an extra look
Check if you need to jiggle
or wiggle that small tin hook.

If you want your toilet tank to refill
jiggle the hook real nice
And then you won't have to wait
should you need to flush it twice.

CHAPTER 15

BEHIND CLOSED DOORS

You all know him, or her. The class showoff, the shameless guest, the gross exhibitionist.

Some psychologists say that the order in which you are born has a great impact on your personality. The youngest in the family, they say, is often the spoiled one, the showoff, and the one most likely to not shut the door when he or she goes to the bathroom. In fact, I was going to write a book entitled, "Birth Orders and Bathroom Odors," exploring the roots of this bad behavior, but I don't think that's necessary. We have the teachings of Confuse-us to guide us.

He once wrote:

> Be modest and humble in all affairs
> Don't let us see your bottom bare.

Okay, Confuse-us did not really care about birth order; he just wanted us to use the bathroom behind closed doors.

What is necessary is this reminder: When you go to the bathroom, whether you're the firstborn, the baby, or the middle of a team of octuplets, just shut and lock the door. No offense, but there are certain times in life when you should *not* be seen or heard. Going to the john is not the time to conduct an open-door policy. Whatever you do in there is strictly your business.

We hope you enjoy yourself to the fullest. But do not infuriate others by taking so long that it keeps them from enjoying their own bathroom experiences. A final note to our wise readers: Now that you're comfortably doing your thing behind closed doors, don't get too comfortable and fall asleep!

You sit in the bathroom, the door is ajar
so everyone close to you knows where you are
To keep the door shut, would show much more class
and keep those you love from sniffing your gas.

When you're in the bathroom
always lock the door
Or else your private business
will become public—that's for sure.

When you're in the restroom
make sure the door is locked and shut
For if it swings open
they'll ogle your butt.

When you're on the potty
doing your duty
Make sure to lock the door
or they'll see your booty.

Life's most intimate moments
are spent upon the toilet
So please lock the door behind you
as viewers would only spoil it.

Don't leave the door wide open
while sitting on the throne
You should be antisocial there
It's best to be alone.

When you're on the can taking a leak
lock the door behind you
or someone may peek.

Never dismiss the sign on the door
Don't go to a room you've not been to before
If you hear ladies screaming
you may not be dreaming
This advice should not be ignored.

When you're in the bathroom
making lots of yellow pee
Always be sure the door is locked
if you value privacy.

Bathroom sounds and bathroom views
are rarely covered by local news
So lock the door and be discreet
as no reporter wants this beat.

You must close the door and mind the hour
before you start singing in the shower.

When you take a shower
sparkling in the buff
Make sure the bathroom door is locked
so you'll be free to strut your stuff.

Wherever you sit on the throne
someone else's or even your own
Hurry to make sure the door is closed
Your poop does not smell like a fragrant rose
It's actually quite flagrant to the nose.

Life can certainly be a bitch
when you have a case of rectal itch
So scratch that itch and scratch some more
Just scratch that itch behind locked doors.

CHAPTER 16

FOR GRACIOUS HOSTS AND HOSTESSES

As you are a person of taste and class, I am sure you take great pride in your home. What a pleasure it is to invite friends over for a grand tour and some Bundt cake and punch. So, congratulations on your immaculate decor, your exquisite sofas and artful paintings, and your "Bless This Humble Home" needlework, which provides just the right touch.

But wait a minute… You haven't neglected your good old bathroom, have you?

When you've been a guest, has a neglectful hostess ever left you and others completely in the lurch by providing you with no toilet paper?

Have you ever visited an otherwise gorgeous home only to find that your hosts have left no guest towels for you and others? And no soap or disinfectant, for crying out loud?

Now, you may indeed want to cry out loud, but you need to handle this in a classy, more dignified way. Never yell at your hosts or go to the extreme of inviting them over just to get revenge.

The great Confuse-us would never approve of that approach. According to one of his most epic teachings, though, it is okay to quietly talk to your host about the situation.

I once went to a lovely home
A big estate of marble and stone
But the bathroom there, to my surprise
Did not have even basic supplies
I told the host he was to blame
He cried, and hung his head in shame.

As a gracious host, you never want to be forced to cry and hang your head in shame. Take the time to ensure that you have your bathroom in perfect working order for your guests. That includes making sure that all parts of the toilet (the lid, the seat, the undercarriage, etc.) will stand up to regular or even rigorous use. Always provide enough guest towels for your visitors. Stock more than enough soap, towels, toilet paper, air freshener, and everything else that will keep your guests happy and coming back for more.

Fix the hinge on your toilet seat
for all your male users
who want to stand and take a pee
and not sit down like losers.

The number one annoyance
is the toilet seat that won't stand
It falls down at the damnedest times
when you cannot free your hands.

You may have to check the hinge on the back
of your good old toilet seat
so your male guests can stand in peace
and not sit in defeat.

You don't want the toilet seat falling down
when you stand up to pee
This may cramp your style
and bring you to your knees.

If your toilet seat doesn't stay up
a man can't take a pee
And so he may be forced to hold
the damn seat with his knee.

A man would like to urinate
in a toilet which cooperates
He cannot aim his stream to pee
if a broken lid cannot stand free.

Ladies, if your toilet seat can stay upright
your man will be overjoyed
You'll avoid a wet and messy sight
and won't have to be so annoyed.

Tighten the screws on the back of the seat
before your guests sit down to doot
That way your guests won't fall off the seat
and you won't be held in ill repute.

Your guest is looking for a towel or tissue
that you as a host have forgotten to issue
So purchase all things you need to buy
and never keep them in short supply.

I pledge allegiance to my guests
that I won't put their patience to the test
I promise to stock up on tissues and towels
to aid them whenever they move their bowels.

When you invite guests to your house
don't leave them in the lurch
Provide plenty of toilet paper
so they won't have to search.

If you're having houseguests over
let me be quite candid
Stock up on tons of TP
or else, they will get stranded.

Never run out of toilet paper
or your guests will have a gripe
And then they'll look for anything
to execute their wipe.

Has a guest ever missed with his tinkle
and there's nothing to wipe up his sprinkle
As a host, you should cover such basic needs
Let the guest mop up his own misdeeds.

Always provide fresh towels
on your bathroom racks
or your guests will have to dry their hands
on their nice clean slacks.

A rude host never checks the rack
to see if there are towels
for their guests to dry their hands
after they move their bowels.

Stock your bathroom with towels
Terry cloth is best
Don't incur the wrath
of every angry guest.

Fancy towels in the powder room
are simply there for show
They look so nice, but don't assume
Use the cheap ones after you go.

If you have house guests visiting
remember your social graces
Leave towels hanging on the racks
for washing their hands and faces.

In some people's homes you could eat off the floor
Others find cleaning such a chore
The bathroom is where the true test lies
Does your guest make it out of the john alive?

When people judge appearance
you can earn *endearance*
Knock your guests right off their feet
by keeping your bathroom nice and neat.

What's the most useful room?
Must be the bathroom, I assume
Furnish and polish and make it exquisite
For a bathroom neglected, folks won't want to visit.

Bathrooms are like soldiers
They like their medals on display
So help them pass inspection
by cleaning them every day.

Your bathroom is under mildew attack
and the little green slime won't give the walls back
Air out the room and wipe down the tiles
to avoid cultivation of little green piles.

When you sprinkle cleanser, remember your goal
Aim the powder down the toilet bowl.

A dirty bowl does not smell well
to those who pass this way
Just put some cleanser in your tank
and your guests might even stay.

Pour cleanser on tiles
Please leave no doubt
Get rid of the odors
and scour that grout.

CHAPTER 17

FOOD-HANDLING ETIQUETTE

This chapter is devoted to, and aimed at, anyone who enters the kitchen or dining room right after using the bathroom. In other words, everyone. So please read on.

Raise your hand if you enjoy cooking. Thank you very much. Now, that we've established who you are, one quick question: How many of you have ever read a cookbook? There are certainly many wonderful cookbooks out there, but I tend to regard them more or less as I do science fiction. They're fun reading, but they don't inspire me to act accordingly.

And none of these cookbooks seem to mention the most important first step, no matter what dish you are preparing. After completing your bathroom experience, wash with soap and hot water, and then dry your hands thoroughly before handling any food. That goes for eating, as well as cooking and serving!

Take it from the great Confuse-us, and his ages-old wisdom. This great bathroom sage enjoyed a good meal, as we all do. He was always meticulous in his food preparation, and he expected the same high standards from anyone who might serve him a meal. He once wrote:

> When done in the bathroom, I certainly hope
> That you wash hands with water and soap
> Before touching food—don't be a dope.

So yes, be like Confuse-us. Be a winner, and clean thoroughly before cooking dinner. (Or before serving or eating any meal.)

If you fancy yourself a foodie
then after you finish your doody
Before you cook, go scrub each finger
No smudge or odor can be left to linger.

I'll say this in the simplest terms
Wash your hands, we don't want your germs.

Peek a boo, we see you
hands unwashed as you leave the loo
On this subject you shouldn't fight us
'cause you could give someone hepatitis.

Don't rush from the bathroom to the kitchen
without being sanitary
Or you might make your loved ones sick
just like good ole Typhoid Mary.

If you wait tables, wash your hands
after you're done in the potty
Or else, you may discover your tips
are especially shoddy.

Food handlers, please honor the moral code
whenever you use the public commode
Do unto others as others do unto you
Washing your hands is the right thing to do.

When you use the bathroom
before cooking food
Just wash your hands
or they'll think that you're crude.

You serve the food, you aim to please
but if you don't wash up, you spread disease
Each little germ or nasty *E. coli*
could be served by you, on wheat bread or rye.

For Employers:

Your employees will serve us with clean hands, we hope
So fix the hot water and stock plenty of soap.

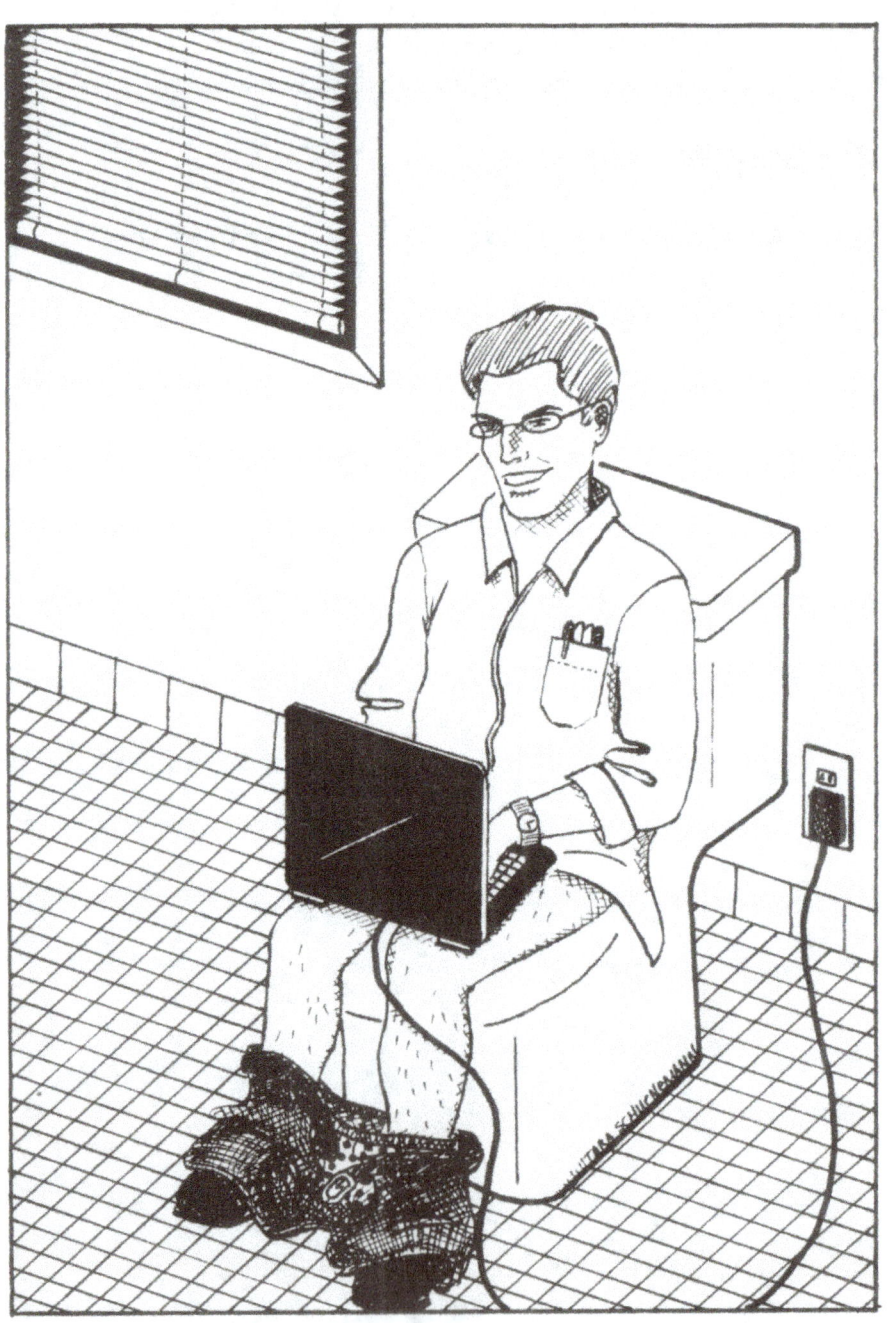

CHAPTER 18

TECHNO-DITTIES FOR COMPUTER GEEKS

A great observer of the modern landscape once wrote, "Smart phones, tablets and PCs are absolute necessities—as indispensable as kitchens, bedrooms and bathrooms." Who was this great observer of the modern landscape? Okay, it was me, and I wrote this very recently. But this statement is true.

Just think about how technology has revolutionized our lifestyles, and even our daily lexicon. Years ago, did we ever concern ourselves with friend requests, Instagram followers or virtual engagement? Did any of the following ever carry double meanings until recently: image resolution, downloads, and product launches? If not, I'm here to help.

There are many similarities between technological terms and words used in the study of bathroom etiquette. These include, but are hardly limited to, downloads, logons, privacy issues and rules for proper transfer protocol. And the less we mention about floppy disks, the better.

Technology is constantly making advances that improve our lives, but our dependence on these improvements often carry a heavy price tag. There is also this: Many of us spend so much time staring at our devices in our rooms that we neglect that other room across the hall—the bathroom. As important as we think our other work and play time are, the bathroom is where we must attend to more necessary, even primal, functions.

Wait a second. Throughout this book, we have looked back at Confuse-us, invoking his sage bathroom philosophy and wisdom that still hold true today. But what might he say about a high-tech world that he could not have anticipated? We do have some clues from a couple of his sayings.

On the *technology* available to him 2,500 years ago, Confuse-us seemed to always want to use the finest.

> If my teachings are to pass the test
> It always pays to buy the best.

At the same time, Confuse-us always warned his disciples not to be workaholics, as this could lead to consequences in the bathroom.

> Work hard, but do not over exert
> Or you'll soon find your bowels hurt.

With all of these considerations in mind, I hope that you will now tear yourself away from social media or your addictive Wordle game long enough to read this chapter. Your work and play will wait for you, and you may be quite relieved (pun intended) later that you took this valuable time out.

> Be moderate in your use of **Java**
> or you'll be dumping loads of lava.

> Your bottom will get very sloppy
> if your toilet **disk** is loose and **floppy**.

> Offending your guests? Avoid that risk
> Don't let them squat on a ***sloppy disk***.

> Don't forget what you learned in computer class
> Cram plenty of **software** up your ass.

> Be careful with your bathroom **browser**
> or you'll end up with one soggy trouser.

> To help you curb your bathroom vices
> limit your time on your **devices**.

If your butt and paunch are filled with raunch
It's time to execute a **product launch**.

In the bathroom, he never did *Excel*
and we all suffered from that smell.

If your stools are getting *Micro-soft*
you must not keep your butt aloft.

After every bathroom trip
flush away each **microchip**.

Flush down all your toilet creations
It's no time for **data visualizations**.

His pee was errant, always short
So his wife called for **tech support**.

A foul odor from a **computer tech**
caused his colleagues to install *smell check*.

If you spend all your time on **X/Twitter**
and instead of flushing, you're just a quitter
your partner may get very bitter.

Always spray the air after you crap
Do it yourself, there is no **app**.

If your bathroom stench just makes you sick
give your spray bottle a **double-click**.

You may be a **computer geek**
but never let your bathroom reek.

Maintain your **privacy**, my brothers
Your *passed-turd* should not be seen by others.

When you **download** big brown **files**
your stench will waft for many miles.

If your rump is feeling plump
it's time to make a **data-dump**.

Your **server** must meet your demands
so tell that person to wash their hands.

Simply flush the handle when your crap smells
You don't need no fancy *whistles and bells*.

Obey proper **transfer protocol**
Don't leave your **downloads** in the bowl.

What would the next user really think
if he **uploaded** your *hyperstink*?

When using another **host's domain**
you must flush all **data** down the drain.

A toilet that is spic and span
is free of **input** when you **scan**.

In terms of a **computer nerd**
a **click** on *flush* will exit turd.

If your toilet's **screen** is flashing brown
your bathroom **monitor** may be down.

If the bathroom smell is not so great
you need to open your **Windows 8**.

If you don't scrub your hands after each wipe
your **mouse** will have good reason to gripe.

The next **user** will be blazing mad
if your cat craps on the **mouse pad**.

If your toilet attracts a lot of traffic
don't make its **resolution** too **graphic**.

When your toilet clogs, don't **double-click**
grab the plunger, get on the stick.

Error message number two
was a failure to flush the loo.

Don't offend your favorite female
Don't **load** her toilet with crappy **email**.

Don't use all your **storage gigabytes**
Delete crap that spoils your appetite.

Your **home page** should make a nice impression
Flush after every toilet session.

Be *computer-and toilet-literate*
Spraying is always considerate.

Most men just find it much too daring
to sit together for some **load sharing**.

Don't let your TP go to waste
Mix and match or **cut and paste**.

It always drives me quite berserk
when my **spreadsheet software** doesn't work.

If your **iPhone** has **low resolution**
flushing it down is no solution.

If you dump too much in the tank
you'll overfill its **databank**.

Forgetting to spray is a disgrace
Don't leave your vapors in **cyberspace**.

It's a **virtual reality**
that in the bathroom **modality**
toilet abnormalities
affect our personalities.

Always follow the **binary code**
Use one and two in the commode.

Don't ever spread a bathroom **virus**
Wipe your butt with the best papyrus.

TARA SCHUENEMANN

CHAPTER 19

ALL ABOUT PET-IQUETTE

If you're a pet lover, as I am, much of your life revolves around your precious pets. Let's discuss the important topic of pet-iquette. Pet-i-who, you ask? I said *pet-iquette*, not *pet-icure*. *Pet-iquette*, quite simply, refers to the behavior necessary to keep your house, especially the john, safe for and from household pets.

So, what exactly are we talking about here? Well, good pet-iquette requires the following safeguards and more:

1. Keeping your litter box clean, smelling relatively tolerable and out of the reach of Fido.
2. Shutting the door to the reading room, so that your favorite honorary family member won't dump in the bathtub or drink from the commode.
3. Letting your pets outside at the appropriate times, so that they might follow good pet-iquette as often, and as soon, as humanly (er, caninely?) possible.

You may be wondering what the great Confuse-us had to say about all this, and here's just a little background. Dogs and cats were domesticated animals in the time of Confuse-us, and in his final years, the philosopher loved to write with his dog (who he affectionately named Pupu) sitting next to his feet. He wrote:

My Pupu brings me so much joy
He is such a wonderful boy
But if my bathroom, I don't control
He'll drink water from toilet bowl.

Confuse-us also loved his wife's two cats, PicLili and Chow Chow, and seemed to take great care of them. He warned:

Your cats will soon get sad and bitter
If you don't keep clean their box of litter.

So, as always, try to be like Confuse-us. Don't allow your litter box to stink to high heaven, even though you had ample opportunity to clean it. You need pet-iquette lessons if your pooch takes drinks from the por-celain bus. And if you own both a cat and a dog, never allow Fido (or Pupu, or whatever you name your dog) to walk around with a cigar in his mouth, courtesy of your litter box.

Give your dog full run of your abode
but always close down your commode.

Fido, keep away from that box
That litter's not a tasty hoagie
It's really not a pleasant sight
to see you chomping on that stogie.

Both cat and man will always gripe
when kitty litter's stale and ripe.

When sharing your bathroom with kitty's litter
a daily scoop will make it fitter.

Never slam the toilet seat
Beware of tiny paws and feet.

THE LEGEND OF CONFUSE-US

Take your pooch outside for a spell
when she has to make a poo
Or your carpet will soon stink like hell
and be adorned with doggy-doo.

A parrot is a lovely bird
sings some of the sweetest notes I've heard
But I'm being serious, not absurd
be careful sweeping up their turds.

The careful cleaning of bathroom floors
protects fur babies that walk on all fours.

If you and kitty bathroom share
do not foul up his humble lair.

A quick spray when kitty has litter gone
stops the odor that lingers on.

When cleaning litter do not slip
and leave behind a gross cat chip.

Beware, even though your cat is grown
in the bathroom lie hazards yet unknown.

On toilet, wisely close the hood
to help your cat survive kittenhood.

A flushed toilet will be your wish
when naughty kitty decides to fish.

A thirsty dog, faithful and true
will be quickly sickened from an unflushed loo.

If litter's too far out of reach
Kitty pet-iquette, your cat will breach.

When you don't watch what your pet devours
prepare for household smells most sour.

A dog you wash and quickly dry
before he shakes and the water flies.

Before you give the dog a bath
close the door and bar his path.

When changing litter, always be sure
to sweep away droppings on the floor.

The wads of hair from the pet you brush
please do not in toilet flush.

If a big mess is made by your ferret
Clean it up, you just have to bear it.

Please make sure not to make the mistake
of eating droppings left by your snake
And never get into the habit
of tasting raisins from your rabbit.

Pet-iquette Song Parody Titles

1. "From the Dogs on the Street Where You Live"
(to: "On the Street Where You Live"—from My Fair Lady)

2. "It Had to be Poop"
(to: "It Had to be You"—Frank Sinatra)

3. "Your Cat"
(to: "My Girl"—The Temptations)

4. "This Tragic Moment"
(to: "This Magic Moment"—Jay and the Americans)

Pet-iquette Song Parodies

1. "From the Dogs on the Street Where You Live"
(to: "On the Street Where You Live"—from My Fair Lady)

I have often walked down this street before
But the excrement was not beneath my feet before.

Always use a scoop to pick up the poop
from the dogs on the street where you live.

2. "It Had to be Poop"
(to: "It Had to be You"—Frank Sinatra)

It had to be you
It had to be you.

I wandered around
and finally found
Your poop on the stoop.

Nobody else gets such a thrill
from taking a poop
under my window sill.

It had to be you
my little dog, Blue
It had to be you!

3. "Your Cat"
(to: "My Girl"—The Temptations)

If you find cat hair
in your toilet bowl
And when you try to flush
it don't go down the hole.

I guess you'll say
What can stop it up that way?
Your cat.
Talkin' 'bout your cat…
Your cat.

If you find cat hair
in your toilet bowl
When it's warm outside
the stuff will start to molt.

I guess you'll pay
or better send your cat away
Your cat.
Talkin' 'bout your cat…
Your cat.

4. "This Tragic Moment"
(to: "This Magic Moment"—Jay and the Americans)

This tragic moment, so different and so new
was like any other 'til your dog doo-doo'd
And when it happened, it took me by surprise
I know that you smelled it, too, by those tears in your eyes.

Smellier than bird doo
Stinkier than my bare toes
It's everything I hated
It almost killed my nose.

This tragic odor, this horrid batch of poo
Will last forever
Forever 'til it kills me and you

Oh-no-no-no (tragic)
Oh-no-no-no (forever)
Oh-no-no-no.

CHAPTER 20

SCOUR YOUR SHOWER, SCRUB YOUR TUB

Few things are worse than taking a shower or bath in an absolutely filthy tub. It kind of ruins my day just thinking about it.

I mean, have you ever taken a bath and had that absolutely helpless feeling of seeing an uninvited species of marine life swimming toward you? You didn't come to an aquarium, did you? At least you didn't have to pay admission, but that's not the point here.

An avid badminton player, Confuse-us belonged to a few clubs for this popular sport. As you might expect from his other teachings, the cleanliness of the bathroom facilities was even more important to him than the condition of the courts. Confuse-us advised:

> Never join a badminton club
> If they don't scrub their showers and tubs.

So, as a good host, remember to always provide a clean bathtub and shower for everyone in your household, and for all your guests. Do not leave so much soap caked on the shower walls or on the floor of the tub that you can't tell what the original color was. And guests, you must also do your part: Clean the shower and tub thoroughly after you are done bathing.

Please, in all your efforts to have a well-stocked, clean-smelling, fine-flushing john, do not ignore your bathtub and shower. You'll be happy that you paid strict attention to them, I'm sure.

Before your guests hit the shower nude
Clean the damn shower, don't be rude
Standing in your grime, they'll feel screwed
and give you lots of attitude.

Leaving hair and soap and grime
in the tub should be a crime
Don't commit this misdemeanor
You must leave the bathroom cleaner.

This above all, to your own tub be true
keep it sparkling, just like new.

You're out of the bathtub, viewing the crime
Hair-filled drain and soap-ringed grime
How can you help this tragic scene?
Be a hero and wipe it clean.

Bubble baths are fun
unless you get too wrinkly
So enjoy the sudsy puffs
but make sure you don't go tinkly.

When you go to take a shower
do you hesitate and glower?
Is there so much drain-clogged hair
that it looks like something died in there?

Keep your bathroom looking fine
clean it 'til it really shines.

Wipe away the soap and grub
that stick to your faithful tub.

After you take your bath
Don't leave dirt and grime in your path
Because after you rub-a-dub-dub
Don't leave a ring around the tub-a-tub-tub.

Isn't it amazing
how the shower will not drain?
But you wouldn't remove the hair clog
unless you had a crane?
Perhaps a handy plunger or a little acid rain?
You really must remove the glump
or just shave off your mane.

The shower's not a swimming pool
Yes, singing in the shower's cool
But please remember, don't get dressed
before you scrub away your mess.

At many a common bath
fungus may cross your path
Your health you can't ignore
wear slippers upon the floor.

If you only use soap that hangs on a rope
deodorant may be your only hope.

The tiles have a nasty way
of building up scum
Wipe them well after you bathe
or else be thought a bum.

TARA SCHUENEMANN

CHAPTER 21

BATHROOM CONTEMPLATIONS

Hopefully, you can see just how important the bathroom is, and how vital proper bathroom etiquette is. This book has conveyed wisdom from the great ancient philosopher Confuse-us and quoted (okay, parodied) other well-known celebrities, musicians, and authors on these very topics.

If you still are not convinced of the bathroom's central role in our lives, let me ask you this. If the bathroom isn't so important, why does it (and the toilet) have more nicknames than any other room in the house? Just think about it for a moment. It's the john, the loo, the privy, the hopper, the office, the library and many more.

The bathroom is our haven, our sanctuary, a place to get away from it all and commune with our personal thoughts. All in the privacy of our own room, and throne.

If your bowels are rumbling while in bed
and your turtle is poking out its head
Go to the bathroom and run like hell
and dump the turtle out of its shell.

When your tummy starts to ache
and your bowels start to shake
Sit on the toilet for heaven's sake
or your undies will look like chocolate cake.

It's that tugging on hair
which makes one not merry
when trying to remove a dingleberry.

Your kind invitation, I'll have to pass
I'm battling severe swamp ass.

If you're not careful on the way to the crapper
your underwear won't be looking too dapper.

Man, what a fart! It had me fainting
and now the walls need some repainting.

When you need time to meditate
as well as time to contemplate
what better place, there's no debate
than the room in which you defecate.

Please be grudging with your fudging
your underwear should not be smudging.

When gas erupts from what you ate
go straight to the privy and flatulate.

Toilet paper may be bought
in white, green, pink, or blue
Yet it is most effective
when it turns a brownish hue.

Put the lid up, and put the seat down
before your butt's painting the color brown.

Flushing a pinched loaf down the head
is the greatest pleasure since sliced bread.

Be a brave man, be a stud
check your own damn stool for blood.

In the proper disposal of feces
lies preservation of the species.

The more food you munge
the more doody you'll plunge.

When properly you wipe your bum
Skidmarks you will overcome.

Because he so finely wiped his backside
in spotless underwear he took much pride.

The bathroom's the place to shower and shave
to sit down and read the book that you crave.

Don't be a sneak, be a proper guest
never snoop in your host's medicine chest.

If the aerosol spray is intoxicating
the musical toilet entertaining
The toilet seat giving joy to your rear
Why would you choose to get out of here?

The secret of bathroom cleaning lies
in knowing how to use your eyes.

Hold onto the handle after you brush
or you may be sorry with what you flush.

Men shave their faces and swab their toes
but always leave hair in their ears and nose.

A word to the wise, a clue to the simple
your face may run red, if you pop that pimple.

It's a sign of beauty and a sign of grace
to rinse off the soap and clean off your face.

My parents always told me
to show true perseverance
So I comb my hair for hours
to make my best appearance.

I flushed some foreign objects
down the hopper late last summer
and I couldn't pay my rent
'cause I had to pay my plumber.

If you want to feel like a disgrace
Wash your feet before your face
But if you want to feel clean and neat
wash your face before your feet.

If you want to see where your body hair goes
explore your belly button and toes.

Tinkling down the toilet
causes lots of slime and grime
That will stain your porcelain bowl
every single time.

The miser skimped on toilet paper
'cause he thought he'd save some bucks
And when he went to wipe one day
he was shit out of luck.

The bathtub yawns, a quiet sea
my end-of-day tranquility
The part of the day that I most treasure
a cruise on senses of total pleasure.

You're relaxing in a bathtub
with soapsuds in your hair
Is there something missing?
How 'bout a scent in the air?
So, no matter how soothing
your bathtub seems to be
there's always something missing
without aromatherapy.

My soap is avocado
My toothpaste is a mint
My conditioner is papaya
that has an orange hint
My bathroom is a potpourri
as if I used a recipe.

Who left the seat up? Who didn't flush?
Why has the soap in the dish become mush?
Where is the toothpaste cap? Who took my comb?
Here in the bathroom, I feel most at home.

GLOSSARY OF BATHROOM TERMINOLOGY

In my efforts to make this book as clear as possible, I have provided a small glossary of some of the jargon and euphemisms that are used throughout the book. As a veteran bathroom user, you may already know many of these terms. To play it safe (a sign of good writing etiquette), I want to make sure that you are now conversant with all of the following terms.

Butt Gravy (a.k.a. Swamp Ass)—A favorite to write about, but alas, no self-respecting person wants this uninvited guest anywhere near them or their undies. Often caused by profuse sweating, it leads to problems (such as rectal itch) that make the simple acts of walking and socializing very treacherous. Compared to butt gravy, skidmarks are a joy to behold.

Courtesy Flush—The first flush, while sitting on the toilet, of a two-flush process. It serves as a courtesy to future users, and/ or anyone else within the vicinity. The courtesy flush prevents noxious odors and the potential overflow. Even if you don't fill the bowl, or you don't think that you have left any visual or nasal evidence, you must courtesy flush. Of course, don't forget the second flush.

Dingleberry—This is not an ice cream flavor or a type of edible fruit. It *is* that little piece of toilet paper (or that little ball of crapola) that continues to hold on for dear life. A dingleberry just dangles from your butt hair like a cling-on.

Porcelain Bus—One of many ways to say toilet. This is a personal favorite, however, and I thought it deserved its own entry.

Power-Dump—Not just any old dump, but a dump of great urgency or prodigious production.

SBD—Silent but Deadly (as in a stealthy fart, that's not heard but carries a pungent odor.)

Skidmark(s)—A very descriptive term that defines the brown trail left in your underwear (the usual place for them), as a result of breaking wind or wiping poorly.

> **Those are some of the unique words that should find their way into every bathroom user's lexicon. Below are some euphemisms for the most common places, actions and functions.**

Defecate—Answer nature's call, crap, doot, drop a deuce, drop a load, dump, grow a tail, have a BM, make a doody, make Number Two, pinch a loaf, play in the sandbox, poo, poop, squat, squeeze out the turtle head, take a dump.

Defecation—Big one, BM, business, caca, cow chip, crapola, doo-doo, doody, droppings, excrement, feces, floater, load, loaf, log, lump, movement, Number Two, poo-poo, poopy, road apple, stool, submarine, turd.

Fart—Backfire, break wind, cut one, cut the cheddar, cut the cheese, cut the salami, let one fly, poot, rip one.

Toilet—(Some of these synonyms may also refer to the bathroom as a whole.)

Amenities, bidet, booth, bowl, can, cat box, chair, chamber of commerce, chapel, chute, comfort station, commode, craphouse, crapper, facilities, happy loop, head, hopper, john, latrine, lavatory, library, little girls' room, loo, office, outhouse, perch, pisshouse, pisspot, poop chair, porcelain bus, pot, potty, powder room, privy, reading room, stall, tank, throne, urinal, water closet.

Urinate—Do Number One, drain the lizard, go, go wee-wee, pee, pee-pee, piddle, piss, powder the nose, take a leak, take a whizz, tinkle, water the garden.

PLOP QUIZ

Thanks again for picking up a copy of my book. I have a great reward for you, a *Plop Quiz*. Now, before you protest, please know that Confuse-us would have wanted it this way.

This great moral philosopher and teacher once said:

> I give quizzes to keep them on their toes
> To see how much each student knows.

Eastern scholars look back on these little tests as the very first known pop quizzes.

Of course, mine is not just any old pop quiz. It's a Plop Quiz, a totally different animal. And a perfectly fun way to test your knowledge of some of the bathroom etiquette lessons you have learned in this book. One final piece of advice. The *questions* will be given *Jeopardy!*-style, so please phrase your *answers* in the form of a question. I hope that makes sense. Oh yeah, feel free to play your own think…I mean…stink music. Hey now!

This is also an open book quiz. You are encouraged to reread the book in order to answer these questions. It's all good, clean fun.

20 QUESTIONS FOR BUDDING

BATHROOM SCHOLARS

(Worth 5 points each—answers on the next page. No peeking.)

1. Often confused with John Fartlett, this more distinguished third cousin of his curated Fartlett's Unfamiliar Quotations.
2. The musical movie that features two different song parodies in this book.
3. For many years, he was Confuse-us's philosophical mentor.
4. The new name for a bathroom etiquette jingle that features the Yiddish language.
5. The term for the first of a two-part flushing process to prevent noxious odors and the occasional overflow.
6. The commandments indicate that this will be the consequence of stuffing too much paper in your duff.
7. This was written on the restroom sign that inspired this book.
8. This has been cited as the number one (that was a minor hint) reason for domestic disputes.
9. In the song parody *Bathroom Man*, this is the affliction Davy suffers from (and probably will for life).
10. Confuse-us's wife was a professional player in this sport.
11. The expression "Hey now!" (not counting this one) can be found this many times in the book.
12. The name of the song category that refers to parodies of country music hits.
13. A common Yiddish word that means to sweat profusely.
14. According to the teachings of Confuse-us, this should happen to a man who doesn't wipe his seat of pee and poop.
15. This is the best way to obey proper transfer protocol of the toilet.

16. This brilliant Swedish scientist invented a scale to measure the amount of stench in a bathroom.
17. According to Confuse-us, *man will have unhappy marriage* if he doesn't do this.
18. The name of the Beatles song parody that references washing hands after using the bathroom.
19. If you don't flush now, you will be doing this later.
20. This uncomfortable state of affairs implies that your posterior has really gotten bogged down.

PLOP QUIZ ANSWERS

1. Who is Fanny Fartlett?
2. What is *The Wizard of Oz*?
3. Who was Confucius?
4. What is a Yingle?
5. What is a courtesy flush?
6. What are dingleberries?
7. What is "If you sprinkle when you tinkle, please be neat and wipe the seat"?
8. What is men not lowering the toilet seat after taking a leak?
9. What is butt gravy?
10. What is Ping-Pong?
11. What is six times?
12. What is Country Dumpin' Classics?
13. What is (to) schvitz?
14. What is "must be banished from the group"?
15. What is to not leave downloads in the bowl?
16. Who is U. R. Reeking?
17. What is clean the undercarriage (of the toilet)?
18. What is "Will You Please Wash Your Hands!"?
19. What is blush?
20. What is swamp ass?

WHAT YOUR SCORE MAY INDICATE

Now that you've completed the Plop Quiz, you may wonder what it all means. Actually, there's no great meaning behind your score, as this quiz was simply devised to be fun.

But since there are levels to everything, here's a scale so you can grade yourself.

(Remember—you get five points for each correct answer.)

0–30 – I suggest you reread the book.

31–60 – You know a whole lot more about bathroom etiquette than people who haven't read this book.

61–80 – Your mastery of bathroom etiquette is quite impressive.

81–100 – You, my friend, are a bathroom etiquette genius approaching the level of the great Confuse-us. I would be most honored to welcome you, and even your power-dumps, inside my bathroom.

A FINAL WORD

I hope that you have enjoyed this book and will place it in the room that you deem the most important to you. You may also want to have a copy in your car for those occasions when you are either a guest in someone's home or traveling for business or pleasure. And don't forget that this book is also available in an e-version for your electronic devices.

Keep this book close at hand if you need a bathroom etiquette tip, crave a laugh or just want to belt out a song parody or two. This book also has Yingles, nursery rhymes, and so much more, including lots of quotes. And you can quote *me* on that.

Which reminds me of this final quote from the great Confuse-us.

> Enjoy your work, enjoy your naps
> Read lots of books, take joyful craps.

You have thousands (or maybe even millions) of bathroom experiences ahead of you. I want all of your future bathroom experiences to be stain-less, painless, happy, and joyfully crappy.

www.ingramcontent.com/pod-product-compliance
Lightning Source LLC
Chambersburg PA
CBHW071722120626
46550CB00001B/341